# Mindfu

CW00523339

*Seven principles to banish stress and boldly
grow your impact, your way*

Anis Qizilbash

First published in 2018 by Anis Qizilbash
anisqizilbash.com

ISBN-13: 978-1724625052
ISBN-10: 1724625055

**If you found this book useful, please leave a review to help
others find it.**

To book Anis to speak at your next conference or bulk
purchase copies of this book contact her at:

Email: a@anisqizilbash.com

Website: anisqizilbash.com

Follow her: @AnisQiz

## ALSO BY ANIS QIZILBASH

*Grow Your Sales, Do What You Love: Mindful Selling for Entrepreneurs and Freelancers*

# TABLE OF CONTENTS

## DEDICATION

My beloved Jennifer, my rock, who always sees the best in me.

For entrepreneurs, freelancers & salespeople everywhere, doing
the challenging work of creating immeasurable value for
individuals and businesses

Imagine for a moment a murky pond with layers of green goo blanketing the surface. Deep within that pond a stem grows, slowly rising through the thick muddy water until it breaks through the surface to reveal a bud that blossoms into a beautiful lotus flower.

The principles offered in this book can help you cut through the muddy waters of fear and the fog of limiting beliefs. My hope is for you to soar above the stress and circumstances pulling you down so you may rise to reveal your brilliant bold self.

*The lotus is born in darkness,*

*but it flowers in the light.*

# Why You Need this Book

If you've picked up this book, chances are you've got a grand vision for your life and to achieve it, you need to be able to sell and influence others. But the thought of selling stresses you out or you lack the confidence to achieve the impact you want to have in the world.

Through seven simple principles, this book addresses the biggest struggle I see people like you face when trying to grow your impact. My deepest hope for you in reading this book is that you start peeling away the layers of fear, lies and deception holding you back from being your best you.

How helpful would it be if you could head off emotional triggers – news headlines, social feeds, or other people – or recover faster when you are triggered? Think about that email that kept you awake at two in the morning or that meeting that slipped through your fingers. We've all been there.

If you could reduce your mind's descent down dark passages of despair from hours or days to minutes, how would your life change?

What difference would strengthening your ability to recover from setbacks or perceived negative experiences, so you could stay focused on what's important, have in your life?

To be clear, I'm not a mindfulness guru or retired monk. Far from it. I still get days where I moan about the postman ringing our doorbell to drop off packages for our whole street. Tech issues trigger my ego as surely as my cat goes crazy for catnip. And nerves can still get the better of me, even though I regularly speak in public.

But thanks to the principles I'm sharing with you, episodes of ego no longer steal my mornings, anxiety doesn't consume evenings and depression no longer derails weekends. I act *despite* being plagued with insecurities and fear. The principles you will learn have helped my clients stop stress consuming them, end fears of selling and combat procrastination so they can grow their business and be a positive impact in the lives of those they love.

## The Pressure Cooker of Life

Let's quickly go back in time, over ten years ago. I had just returned from a three-day trip to Spain, meeting with new prospects I'd cold called a month before.

My boss called me into his tiny cubby hole office and said, "Anis, I'm afraid I'm going to have to give you a warning. The powers above expect £5k a week. It's been seven weeks without revenue. We're giving you one month and if you don't bring in £30,000 we're going to have to let you go."

My heart sunk and my throat tightened as if a snake were slowly squeezing the life out of me.

"But we had Christmas break in between, and the product isn't out until April."

"I'm afraid it's policy. Employees usually only get four weeks, but you got an extra cushion."

Before accepting the job, colleagues had warned me; this company had impossible expectations of their salespeople, didn't support them and easily sacked them. I even brought up this question during the interview. I ignored the warnings. Desperation to get back into the UK job market after living abroad for almost four years influenced my decision to take the first job offered.

Faced with the prospect of getting sacked, I could have made so many excuses: my client base was rubbish, the other salespeople had all the best clients, most of my client-base never spent with us, most never heard of us, there's no marketing support, our product is seasonal, not monthly or weekly, so why are we measured with same metrics as all the other salespeople working on different products. But excuses would have gotten me nowhere. The fact remained, if I didn't bring in £30k in a month, I was out.

To gather myself, I stepped out for a coffee. Instead, a tidal wave of stress crashed down on me. If I didn't make this target I would be out of a job. My confidence and self-belief would be in the gutter. Selling myself into a new sales job in that state would be impossible. No one would hire me. My career and life would be over. I burst into ugly tears and choked because I couldn't cry enough. How did I get here? What was the point? I went down a dark road very quickly, which was easy for me back then having wandered into the thicket of depression.

That evening, I resolved to put my head down and do the best I could. Four weeks later, at noon on deadline day, a £25k booking-order crept through the fax machine, bringing up my total revenue to £29,300. It was enough to let me off the hook.

After almost nine years in sales, my sales skills were not enough to help me through that scenario because I was overwhelmed by the pressure cooker of stress in my head. Selling when you're filled with fear will never bring you the results you want, and it makes for an awful experience for every prospective customer you encounter.

It was critical to root out the stress so I could focus and strategize on how to achieve the goal. I had to clear my head of fear so I could walk tall in prospect meetings instead of cowering in desperation. The clock was ticking and I had to be my best in every moment.

The pivotal moment for me was deciding to work on my mindset. I wondered why bad things kept happening to me. Toxic personal relationships. Pervasive conflicts with colleagues. Hostile work environments. What was the common denominator? Me. Instead of tinkering with external elements like my body or my environment, I decided to deal with my inner self.

I submerged myself in research. I recognised how my fear states impacted my daily decisions, from what I said to prospects to how ideas flowed to me and my body language in meetings. *My mindset impacted absolutely everything.* Crucially, I became aware that I rarely performed as my best self while filled with fear.

I'm not talking about transforming into a chest-thumping, adrenaline-fuelled gorilla-tearing-everything-in-its-way-to-get-what-it-wants. That's not me. I mean becoming focused and flowing; inspired and impassioned; centred and certain. When I'm in these states, I get stuff done. People and ideas show up, timing is perfect and I get the best results. Things feel *easier*. Hard work doesn't feel hard, it feels purposeful. More importantly, I'm funnier.

## The Price of Excess Baggage

Another thing weighing me down at the time was a tonne of

personal baggage. Having struggled with addiction in the past, I was depressed, frequently taking sick days around weekends to spend four days in bed. I spent my spare time reading everything I could get my hands on – cognitive psychology, neuroscience, mindfulness, self-help, behavioural psychology, etc. I sought therapy and attended courses.

Applying what I learned, I felt fully alive for the first time I could remember. It seemed to work for others too. During conversations with friends, topics veered to personal struggles and stress. After I shared a few tips, they found solace right there, in that moment. I had always enjoyed helping others in sales and business, but from that point on I became obsessed with helping people with their mindset struggles. It gives me the highest of highs.

## Where Are You Now?

Is the version of you that you present in front of prospective clients your grandest you or is there more?

On a scale of one to ten, how would you rate your level of engagement in your business and life?

If your number wasn't a ten, why didn't you pick a higher number? Is it because you know there's more inside of you that wants to be expressed, to give and serve and create a bigger impact?

I want to help you create your bigger impact, but I want to help you to do it *your* way. Not my way, not the salesy seller way, but *your* way. But you can't grow your impact if you don't believe in your value. If you don't believe in your value, you can't possibly convince others of your value. The loftiest logic or most exhaustive research will never help you sell yourself or your ideas if you're filled with fear or self-doubt. You cannot give what you don't have.

13

*Startups and starting out*

For the new business owner, self-employed and those in non-typical sales roles, sales activities often trigger fear, stress and avoidance. You could learn all the sophisticated sales and persuasion techniques and tactics ever invented, but they're useless if you can't make the first move. Sitting in front of your McDreamy prospect is a wasted opportunity when your nerves take over and memory flakes on you. Knowing refined methods doesn't make you act; you must still pick up the phone, send the email, or attend the event. And knowing what to say is useless when a wall of fear stands in your way.

*Seasoned pros*

For seasoned sellers, technology holds your attention hostage and drives you to distraction. There's plenty of research showing distraction makes you take longer to complete tasks and degrades the quality of your work. One study published in the *Journal of Experimental Psychology*[1] shows even three-second distractions, like silencing a buzzing phone, doubled the error rate in tasks, while four- second interruptions tripled error rates! Another major source of distraction are your emotions, triggered by external events, like stressing about emails or ruminating about annoying people. These emotions can keep you up at night or make you unpleasant company for friends and family.

# How Is this Book Different?

First, I'm not going to spend any time on sales strategies, tactics, or techniques, since I already wrote book about that called *Grow Your Sales, Do What You Love: Mindful Selling for Entrepreneurs and Freelancers.* Furthermore, techniques and strategies are like palliatives, solutions that treat symptoms rather than causes. Imagine for a moment you've got a recurring chesty cough. Every time it rears its noisy head, you treat it with cough medicine. The cough medicine might stifle the cough for a few hours a day and let you sleep more restfully at night, but it won't stop you getting a cough in the future. You'd need to make changes in your diet and lifestyle to prevent chesty coughs in the future.

This book aims to address the *cause* of the stress and strife that get in the way of your business and life. The focus is helping you to be proactive, by working on your mindset. It's easy to get caught up on smarter questioning, data-led lead generation or the hottest social selling tactics, but everyone has access to these ideas. It is your mind that lets you execute (or procrastinate), stay the course (or veer into the media wormhole), stand out and be at your best (or worst).

Second, this book is not about "fake it 'til you make it" audacity. I much prefer being authentic, flaws and all. It's far too difficult trying to be someone else. And it's not about adopting a different persona and hiding who you are. If you're not endowed with an "abundance of confidence" like most salespeople you've met, then the words and techniques they use won't sit well with you. Your fear of speaking up, appearing rude, being pushy, feeling greedy or unworthy stops you dead in your tracks. Fear is like a zipper on your lips muting your words. You reject yourself before you let prospects hear what you have to say. It's about being more of the brilliant you that lies hidden deep inside you.

Third, this book is not about positive thinking or burying your head in the sand, pretending everything is fine when it's clearly not just to avoid stress. It's about fundamental timeless principles, grounded in neuroscience favoured by elite Olympian athletes and backed by centuries of wisdom, to help you let go of the junk holding you back.

You have everything inside you. You have all the power you need. It's already there. I've seen it. I've noticed this through 1-to-1 coaching and delivering workshops with people like you who fear and hate selling and by working on my own emotional baggage. One lady who attended my workshop was laid off at the age of 55. She couldn't see beyond her recent circumstances to appreciate how her three decades of experience could be of tremendous value to others; instead, she believed she was doomed. But after a few tweaks using principles you'll learn in this book, a twinkle of hope emerged in her eyes, a resolute strength reappeared in her tone.

Layers of false beliefs and ideas have blocked you from taking action to grow your impact. But it ends now.

## How to get the most out of this book

This book is presented in a way I hope helps the principles stay with you long after you put the book down. They are illustrated through real-life examples – fictionalised to protect client privacy – blended with practical wisdom.

You decide how you read this, but one thing I insist is that you please have a go at the exercises. Otherwise, it is like reading about exercise but never doing the exercise. The only way you will gain any benefit from your investment reading this book is by doing the practical exercises in each chapter.

Knowledge is *potential* power. Action turns knowledge into power.

We'll start with debunking the myths that stop you from being your true self, then take a quick tour of the main players driving your behaviour. This will pave the way to understanding why the principles work before we get into the seven principles themselves.

# Empty Your Cup

*Self-confidence is not a feeling of superiority, but of independence.*
- Lama Yeshe, Tibetan lama

*Courage in an untrained mind leads to cruelty, and in a trained mind it leads to hope and compassion.*
- P.J. Saher, author and philosopher

*When I let go of what I am, I become what I might be.*
- Lao Tzu, founder of Taoism

O nce upon a time, during the Meiji era (1868 – 1912) a Japanese Zen Master named Nan-in received a university professor visiting to inquire about Zen. Nan-in served the professor tea, pouring until the professor's cup was full. Instead of stopping, he kept on pouring.

The professor watched politely, trying to hide his dismay at the overflowing cup. He couldn't hold back any more and said, "But, it is overfull. No more will go in."

"Like this cup," Nan-in said, "you are full of your own opinions and speculations. How can I show you Zen unless you first empty your cup?"

## Your Cup of False Beliefs Runneth Over

Like that over-flowing cup, a mind filled with beliefs and opinions cannot contain new ideas until those thoughts are emptied. *Empty what thoughts?* you might be wondering. Popular myths and misconceptions about confidence that may be stopping you from fulfilling your potential. Here are some examples:

*Myth: I need to be talkative and outgoing.*

People prefer hearing themselves talk over listening to others, so not being talkative works in your favour because you leave more space for others to talk.

*Myth: I need rhino-thick skin. Rejection bounces off confident people like a fly bouncing off a closed window.*

You don't need rhino skin to deal with rejection, just the ability to reframe the meaning of rejection. Aim for the non-resistance of tai chi as opposed to the rock-hard abs of mixed martial arts.

*Myth: I need a personality transplant to be confident.*

Confidence is not a personality trait. It's a state of mind; you can activate a state of mind the way you activate fear or excitement.

*Myth: I have to be assertive and aggressive.*

Persistent and resourceful, yes; forceful and manipulative, definitely not. Aggression and force are signs of deep weakness, not steady strength.

*Myth: To be confident I already need to be good at selling and communicating, but I can't be good at it if I'm not confident. It's a classic chicken-and-egg situation.*

Confidence comes from faith in your ability to figure out what you need to do and then doing it.

*Myth: Confidence is something you're born with. You have it or you don't.*

A study of twins raised in similar environments debunks this natural predisposition argument.

## Nature versus nurture debunked

Robert Plomin, a renowned behavioural geneticist at London's

King's College, conducted an ambitious study that followed 15,000 sets of twins from birth to adulthood. Studying twins is the most effective method for debunking the nature-versus-nurture mystery because it gives researchers the ability to compare genes (nature) with environmental (nurture) influences on the development of traits or disorders. After taking a closer look at confidence he discovered,

> The student's self-perceived ability rating was a significant predictor of achievement, even more than IQ. Put simply, confidence trumps IQ in predicting success.

This research says that gaining more knowledge doesn't guarantee confidence and success. It also tells us confidence isn't a natural trait bestowed upon the lucky few; it can be nurtured by anyone. Confidence isn't just about saying you're perfect and whole just the way you are or claiming you can do whatever you put your mind to either. The research tells us our *belief* in our ability determines our success.

Famed Stanford professor of psychology Albert Bandura has a theory about self-belief called *self-efficacy theory*. His theory states that confidence is your belief in your ability to take action, and the most effective way of cultivating a strong sense of self-belief is through *mastery experiences*[2], which are successful experiences of mastering a task or controlling an environment. Consistently taking action and achieving small wins build a solid foundation for belief in your ability because you begin to perceive yourself as a success instead of a failure. The more you believe, the more action you take, and the greater the momentum you build. Confidence is not a natural state, but a feeling closely linked to sustained action.

How often does a lack of confidence in one area spread to other areas of your life? Here are two important things for you to remember:

*Doubt, inaction and indecision feed fear.*

*Action is the antidote to fear.*

But how can you act when you're weighed down with self-doubt? Awareness is the path to transcending your obstacles; you cannot overcome what you cannot see. This book will show you how to peel away the issues pulling you down, so you can take decisive action.

# Living Under the Influence

Participants in a Yale department of psychology experiment were asked to hold a cup of coffee. Half held a hot cup and the other half, an iced cup, for about 10 to 25 seconds. The participants were then asked to read a cover story article and complete a questionnaire about the character in the article. Those holding the hot coffee cup were significantly more likely to rate the person's character in the story as warm and friendly than those holding the iced drink. In other words, the temperature of the coffee affected perception.

In another study published in the *Journal of Experimental Psychology*, researchers had participants play a simple betting card game (e.g. Blackjack) on a computer. After they were dealt two cards, a word related to betting or passing flashed across the computer screen. The researchers told participants that the word was purely a distraction and not intended to be informative. Yet participants were more likely to bet when primed with bet-related words, especially when the value of their cards was ambiguous. The researchers concluded:

> Even when individuals know that a particular stimulus is irrelevant for the task at hand, exposure to that stimulus can set processes in motion that bias our behaviour in unintended ways.[3]

These experiments show how easily and constantly we are influenced by our environment.

# Bias and Trip-Wires and Snares, Oh My

If you are unconsciously influenced by external events and circumstances, it will be difficult, at best, to achieve the results you want in life. But it's not just external clues subtly manipulating you; your internal monologue is influencing you all the time.

## The enemy within

How often have you snapped at your colleague or spouse when you were stressed only to regret it later? How often does fear of making that call or attending that networking night divert your attention to far more "important" activities like commenting on Facebook or "researching" on Youtube? How frequently does lack of confidence scare you from asking for the sale or increasing your fees, compelling you to discount your pricing before the other person even asks? You know what you need to do, but your mind gallops away to a dark and desperate place, rendering you powerless.

*Negative feedback loop of thoughts*

Stress, fear and the desire for ease massively influence your decisions and actions, and those decisions rarely serve your best interest. Your brain has a bias towards short-term pleasure. Most of us would prefer to take £20 today rather than wait and pocket

£25 next week or drink an extra glass (or three) of wine, instead of refraining and enjoying a clear head in the morning. This bias towards the short-term gain keeps us from acting in our own best interest.

Perceived day-to-day psychological dangers like networking when you hate it, sales meetings when you've never done it before, pitching five mean looking investment bankers or cold calling for the next two hours are typical triggers of stress. If you constantly mistakenly believe you're in danger, you continually trigger your body's stress response, shifting resources toward fighting off life threats or fleeing from danger. You can't boldly move forward when you're defensively holding back.

Your ability to control your attention is your most exquisite resource because from your thoughts everything is born. Addiction to distraction stifles your ability to focus, erodes your confidence and weakens your resilience. The result? You're reactive instead of proactive, reflexive instead of reflective. You participate in the effect instead of controlling the cause. Your ability to direct your thoughts influences how you cope with stress, make decisions and effect change.

*Positive feedback loop of thoughts*

considered
thought

conviction
& certainty

courageous
action

compelling
results

# Are You the Passenger or the Driver?

You have this illusion that you're in control but you're not. You're chauffeured around by that voice in your head. Here are some common thoughts stopping you from growing your impact:

*If I contact people to sell, it looks like I'm not doing very well. They will think I'm desperate and my business is failing.*

*The person I'm calling is minding their own business and I'm going to bother them.*

*My industry is small and if one person feels insulted with me selling to them, they will talk to other people in the industry.*

*I don't like people disturbing me, so I don't want to bother them.*

*Selling is beneath my dignity; I shouldn't have to ask.*

*Someone else should do the selling for me, it's not my job.*

*They'll say my services/products cost too much.*

*They'll say my offering is not innovative enough.*

*What if they don't like me?*

*What if this doesn't work?*

*What if I say the wrong thing?*

*What if they say no?*

*What if they're rude?*

*What if they think my offering is rubbish or not good enough?*

What story does your internal monologue weave? Stop for a moment and consider it.

Telling you what to say might sound like a good temporary fix, but that's dealing with the world of effects. Knowing smooth techniques doesn't make you pick up the phone. You still have to send that email, make the call or attend the meeting, which is where your internal monologue stops you. The world inside you is the cause, the world outside, the effect. To change your external circumstances, you must first change the cause.

Now that you're aware you're living under the influence of external and internal priming, you have a choice and with choice comes power. When you see how you're being influenced by external and internal forces you can decide between maintaining the status quo or doing something about it.

You're still here so I'm guessing you want to repossess your power. In the next chapter, we dig a little deeper to discover what moves you. Understanding is the seat of power; when you understand what moves you, you can be proactive instead of reactive.

# Know Thyself

*If you know the enemy and know yourself, you need not fear the result of a hundred battles.*
- Sun Tzu, Chinese General and philosopher

*The fact that the body is lying down is no reason for supposing that the mind is at peace. Rest is... far from restful.*
- Seneca, Roman philosopher

*Your own Self-Realization is the greatest service you can render the world.*
- Ramana Maharshi, Indian sage

There is a well-known Zen story about a man sitting on top of a wild galloping horse. A man watching from the roadside asked, "Where are you going?" to which the man on the horse replied, "I don't know! Ask the horse!"

Our minds are that galloping horse, taking us goodness knows where. To understand why, let's take a peek inside your grey matter, so when the going gets tough, you can challenge your desire to give up.

## Four Modes of Thought

Technological advances in the 1990's allowed neuroscientists to see what was happening in the brain in real time, transforming their understanding of our neural activity. We'll look at just two parts of the brain that influence your actions because only when you're aware of them can you control them.

A significant part of how you perceive the world comes from inside your head. Your mind has four default modes, which will do one of four things[4] when left on autopilot:

1. Sports Presenter: Commenting, play-by-play, the action of your own life
2. Marty McFly: Travelling through time, rehashing the past and playing out an imagined future

3. Me Me Me: Analysing what the present moment means for your sense of self
4. Constant Comparator: Caught up in thoughts of comparing yourself to others

Any of these modes sound familiar? When you're walking (and not on your phone), which of the four modes does your mind fall into? What about when others are talking?

Take note, that's your mind's default mode. When you recognise it, you can do something about it.

# Why We Are The Way We Are

To help you understand why you suffer from stress, distraction and anxiety, we'll take a quick bird's-eye view of our brain's function in the greater context of human evolution before zooming in.

Only a few thousand years ago humans lived as hunter-gatherers. We didn't have mortgages, TVs or advertisers telling us we're incomplete without buying this or that product. In the grand scheme of our species' evolution, more change has occurred in the past 300 years than in the previous 1000 years combined. To experience the same amount of change we've gone through in the past 300 years, you'd have to take your time machine back 12,000 years to the agricultural revolution, to a time when humans ceased their nomadic ways and became sedentary. It was only with the advent of agriculture that we started thinking about the future, worrying about weather, food availability and protection of land. Yet because of the slow nature of evolution, we continue to operate with the same brain as our hunter-gatherer ancestors.

Let's look at the main players in your brain driving your day-to-day behaviour.

## The Hammer, a.k.a. your fear centre

The ancient core of our brain is the limbic system. It lies deep within the brain and it is central to our emotions. According to professor of psychiatry Daniel Siegel[5], it essentially deals with one question: "Is this good or is this bad?" We advance towards the good and retreat from the bad.

Within this limbic system is the almond-shaped amygdala, associated with aggression, anxiety, automaticity and fear. It triggers our automatic survival response: flee, fight or freeze. When my wife let out a blood-curdling scream after seeing what she thought was a spider crawling down her face (it was her own hair), it was the Hammer in action. The Hammer is constantly on guard, operating beneath our conscious awareness, ready to strike with blinding swiftness. But as Abraham Maslow stated, "If all you have is a hammer, everything looks like a nail." As a hat tip to Maslow, we will call the amygdala "the Hammer".

During the days of our hunter-gatherer ancestors, when life was fraught with physical danger, the Hammer kept us alive. But our brain reacts to psychological stress the same way it responds to life-threatening physical danger. It lands us in trouble, causing us to do or say things we later regret.

The Hammer gets riled up by unnerving social circumstances and uncertainty[6] – perhaps when you're selling. Maybe it's a letter from the tax collector, detainment by law enforcement or an approach from a salesperson that sparks the Hammer for you. It can be triggered by innate fears – mostly physical dangers such as falling or dying – and learned fears, which are mostly psychological. The Hammer injects suspicion and vigilance into decision making in social settings, which explains your distrust of salespeople.

All things being equal, the Hammer reacts more powerfully to perceived negative events than to positive ones. Psychologists call this negativity bias, and media providers, movie makers and marketers know this, which is why newsrooms follow the dictum, *if it bleeds it leads*. Trauma and negative events attract more attention and clicks than positive events. Also, we are more likely to respond to or learn from negative information.

It's not all bad. The brain's negative bias served as a critical evolutionary function for humans, but in the modern world, where life-threatening danger isn't an everyday thing, the Hammer generates undesired consequences.

How often do you snap at loved ones, criticise colleagues or scold strangers only to regret it later?

How regularly do you stress about stuff, get offended at comments or resent it when rivals brag?

The force and regularity of emotional arousal by psychological fears is a chronic health and performance hazard.

## The Coach, a.k.a. your drill sergeant

On the outer layer of your brain you'll find the prefrontal cortex. Its range of expertise includes working memory, self-control, strategic organisation of knowledge, executive decision-making, long-term planning, emotion regulation, governing impulsivity, activating willpower and initiating action. Quite an impressive portfolio, eh? The Coach is a fitting name for the prefrontal cortex as it makes you do the harder thing when it's the right thing to do instead of lapsing into "easier" habitual behaviour.

The Coach tells you to wake up now instead of snoozing or to go to the gym instead of watching another hour of TV. It helps you focus on writing that email, perform sales activities instead of faffing on social media and recall critical information that helps you nail meetings. Essentially, it allows you to delay gratification and take decisive action toward your goals.

## 90 seconds to clarity

When neuroscientist Jill Bolte Taylor suffered a stroke she lost the functions of the left side of her brain, the source of the ego, judgement and incessant chatter. She explains in her wonderful memoir, *My Stroke of Insight: A Brain Scientist's Personal Journey*[7], what happens when you have a thought that triggers a strong emotional response.

> Within 90 seconds from the initial trigger, the chemical component of my anger has completely dissipated from my blood and my automatic response is over. If, however, I remain angry after 90 seconds have passed, it's because I have chosen to let the circuit continue.

One time my anger was triggered when our cat Whiskey scratched the sofa while I was editing this manuscript. I had already kicked her out of the room and let her back in six times. The surge of anger washed over me but evaporated after 90 seconds. Since I was timing this, I was aware of what I was thinking and continued working in a calm state. I recognised that in the past, the anger continued because I egged it on with thoughts like, *She's doing this on purpose, why doesn't she listen?*

*90 Seconds to clarity*

The beauty of Taylor's insight is that you have a 90-second window to decide: "Do I want to continue feeling down and pump more poison into my body or do I want to be healthy and feel good?" Deciding which thought you chose in the next moment dissolves the triggered response, putting you in control.

# The Perpetual Stress We Don't Notice

Let's imagine something you perceive as bad happens. Maybe you don't have any prospects and you're worried how you'll pay your team. Or your boss says you've got to generate £200k in two months. These scenarios trigger the Hammer, which inhibits your calm states and mobilises stress states, releasing chemicals that increase the force and rate of your heartbeat.

During the stress response, your body's long-term renovations, like tissue repair, growth, healing and cell reproduction, are postponed until after the crisis. But when you're worried or angry, how long does the emotion stick around? Hours? Days? Maybe even weeks? And how often are you triggered with fear and worry? During these extended periods of stress, your body isn't maintaining itself as it should, and this weakens your immune system.

When the Hammer activates the lifesaving stress response, not only are your repair functions inhibited but your working memory is hijacked, your creativity is stifled, your judgement is impaired, your attention is splintered, and your confidence is shattered. Operating from survival mode does nothing to help you perform at your best or soar to new heights.

### Who's guiding the horse?

Our minds are like a galloping horse, taking us to an uncertain destination. But now that you know the four default modes of your mind, you have a clue as to where the horse is taking you.

You met two characters influencing your behaviour. The Hammer asks, "Is this good or is this bad?" then reacts accordingly. The Coach makes you do the harder thing when it's the right thing to do. You also know that when you are automatically triggered, you have a 90-second window to take control.But who is guiding the horse? In the next chapter, we learn about the first principle, which will help you take back control of the reins.

# PRINCIPLE I

# Make Space to Watch

*When your whole attention is focused on the razor edge between silence
and noise, when silence becomes a sound, it's now.*
– Ruth Ozeki, author and Zen Buddhist priest

*The past has no power over the present moment.*
– Eckhart Tolle, spiritual teacher

*You cannot prevent the birds of worry and care from flying over your head.
But you can stop them from building a nest in your head.*
– Chinese proverb

Faiz was on his way to a prospect meeting, a phone pressed to his ear. Another day of back-to-back meetings. He tried to make the most of each minute by ending calls as he rushed into the next meeting. Hours later, waiting in the reception for another meeting, he was on the phone again. The clock was ticking for his new business. Securing investor money before competitors caught up with his offering occupied every corner of his mind.

Faiz carried his splintered energy into every encounter; while he was physically in the meeting, his mind was elsewhere, replaying the conversation from ten minutes earlier. He thought about what he should have said, the potential outcome of the call and what needed to be done next. In prospect meetings he robotically repeated his spiel, never noticing if others were engaged. He did not notice the glazed eyes of the people opposite him or the fact that the person at the end of the table was staring at his own shoes. If Faiz noticed their attention falter, he would talk louder, faster and with greater urgency, hoping his efforts would force them into submission.

Faiz was permanently where he'd just been or where he should be, but rarely where he *actually* was. This absent-from-the-present-moment mindset can result in missing opportunities sitting in front of you or failure to receive inspiration. What's the point of investing energy in setting up meetings when you're rarely in the meeting?

# Where Are You?

You are wherever your attention is. It doesn't matter where you are physically, it's where you are mentally that matters. You experience whatever your attention focuses on. You could be on a beach in Bali, coconut with a straw in one hand, delicious novel in the other, but if you're wondering about your social media feed, what your boss said last week or prospects you need to chase up, then you're not really on the beach, much less on holiday. You're in your mental location, not your physical location. You are wherever your mind is.

When someone talks to you while you're thinking of an interesting thing to say, you're not listening. In a fraction of a second, your body language shows the other person you're not listening. We know when you're not listening. The biggest tell-tale signs are glazed eyes or an ill-timed nod. That's you trying to disguise the fact that you're not listening or so deep in thought you are unaware of your actions. How do you feel when you know someone isn't listening to you? Now imagine how that makes the other feel.

When you're thinking, i.e. not being present, you cannot hear what the person in front of you is saying. You might catch the odd word, but you miss the gist of their expression, which leads to misunderstanding and missed opportunities. To compensate (and make matters worse), you talk instead of inquiring.

Thinking about where you were or where you should be fractures your attention, dims your perception and clogs your inspiration. Above all, it makes the other person feel bad. You win people over and build trust by understanding them and making people feel good about themselves, not by ignoring them and thinking about yourself.

### Woodpecker, meet brick wall

When stressed, we often revert to autopilot, repeating habitual behaviours even though the action is ineffective. For example, the other day I had a tech-related issue with my website. I did the same thing over and over, faster and faster, getting more frustrated. Fortunately, my wife was sitting nearby and reminded me to breathe. After taking a breath, I made a chink of space between me and the problem, allowing room for a solution. An overactive Hammer clogs access to the Coach, disabling your ability to recognise what's not working and explore a new strategy. In survival mode, your brain tells you to repeat the old pattern of behaviour like a woodpecker on a brick wall.

What does this have to do with growing your impact? Your impact is determined by your influence. Your influence is determined by your actions. Your actions are directed by your emotions. Your emotions are governed by your thoughts. Understanding the internal mechanics of how you create external impact helps you enhance your performance while mitigating the menacing behaviours pulling you down. Understanding yourself empowers you to direct yourself and others.

# Mindfulness as Collapsing Time

The first principle is about collapsing time so you can make space. Eliminate the past and future so you can be in the moment. Imagine you're en route to a meeting and your mind rehashes a conversation from last week or worries about a developing issue that is out of your control. Neither of those moments exist right now; one is from last week, the other is a projection of the future. When gripped by the default thoughts your mind generates, you miss the magic unfolding before you.

### A trend or timeless practice?

To collapse time, first you need to be aware of where your

attention is; this is also known as mindfulness. Naysayers dismiss mindfulness as another fad, nothing more than trending nonsense. The definition of a fad is wild enthusiasm for a short-lived craze. Pokémon Go was a short-lived craze. Women wearing jumpsuits was a fad. I had one in the '80s and I loved it so much that I kept wearing it after a growth spurt. I had to over to make it fit! These things are fads. Mindfulness, on the other hand, is an ancient practice that's been around for over 2000 years.

Some dismiss mindfulness as a religious practice. It has its roots in Buddhism and other religions encourage a similar practice of prayer, which directs one to shift attention away from the usual day-to-day ruminations to something bigger. But it is essentially a tool. Most religions encourage giving alms to the poor. Does that mean helping those in need is a "religious" activity? Of course not. Mindfulness is just a vehicle used to express a state of being and a way of living. Furthermore, elite Olympic athletes use mindfulness to let go of stress and get into flow states of peak performance.

Detractors say mindfulness causes more harm and increases anxiety in people. My first awakening – a gap of silence in the stream of thoughts – did bring me stress in the days and weeks that followed because I was suddenly aware of this gushing river of thoughts in my mind I had never before noticed. I had to stop them. If I didn't, I'd get depressed again. I experienced a panic attack from this worry. But by sticking to my daily practice, I learned to tame the river of thoughts and not get pulled under.

## But what is mindfulness?

What is mindfulness, exactly? According to Dr. Jon Kabat-Zinn, creator of the Stress Reduction Clinic and the Centre for Mindfulness in Medicine and widely known as the guy who popularised mindfulness in the West, defines it as "paying attention in a particular way; on purpose, in the present moment, and non-judgmentally". I also like author of *Emotional Intelligence* Daniel Goleman's definition:

> Mindfulness is a method of training your attention, so you can bring it where you want and keep it where you want.

What does this mean? It boils down to being aware of where your attention is focused. Are you gripped by your thoughts or are you truly experiencing where you are?

Returning to this idea of a gushing river of thoughts, imagine a fish swimming in a river; they don't notice the water. It's just there, all around them, all the time. Suppose you point out the water to them. The water was there all along but suddenly they can't help but notice it. The same idea applies to your thoughts; you're so consumed by them that you don't notice, until you are made aware of them.

Perceiving pulls you out of the darkness of your thoughts into the light of the present moment. When you watch your thoughts, which activates the Coach, you have a choice: continue being arrested by them or find release. If you could stop negative thoughts from ruining your life, what difference would that make?

## Finding a breath

The single biggest obstacle to experiencing this so called *present moment* is identifying with your thoughts. Like a gushing river, your thoughts pull you under, drowning you in the past or future and everything that's missing in your life, triggering the Hammer. You activate the stress state where your breath becomes shallow, your heart races and you tense up all over. You are literally gasping for breath.

When you step out of the river of thoughts, there is no past or future. You have collapsed time. Are you ready to step out of the river and make space to catch a breath of air?

You can do this exercise anywhere. Inhale and exhale a little louder than usual and listen to your breath. Go on, do it now. Put the book down. Take one deep inhalation and a slowly exhale, all the while listening to your breath.

Done it? Good. Have another go, but this time do it twice. Listen to your breath. Feel your belly rise and fall. Sometimes you can hear your heartbeat too.

*INHALE*

*EXHALE*

*INHALE*

*EXHALE*

How was that?

Perhaps you're thinking, *Yes, I can breathe. So what, I'm still here; I still have a ridiculous target, the sky is still grey, my cat is still dead and I still haven't sold anything!*

## The reward

When listening to your breath, you're not gripped by your thoughts because you can't think and focus on your breath at the same time. Paying attention to your breath is like stepping out of the river for a few seconds.

When the dark clouds of stress and worry descend, they can stick around for hours and, quite often, days. These worrisome thoughts reinforce the Hammer, flooding your body with the stress chemical cortisol, constraining your creativity, inhibiting your insight and impeding your recollections. No wonder you can't remember obvious things during meetings or calls, like why your offering is unique or why your last client loved working with you.

Making space to be aware of your thoughts and where your attention is gives you the choice of whether you want to be swept along the current or not. Stepping out of the river brings you into the present moment. See how this has nothing to do with religion or fads? It's not about being empty of thoughts but being aware of them.

## How many sounds can I hear?

Here's another exercise you can do at home or on the go.

Right now, listen to the sounds around you. Be aware of the tiniest of noises you can sense. For example, I can hear two different birds tweeting; cars driving; the patter of this keyboard; the distant whoosh of an airplane; and my cat snoring, the cutest sound ever!

How many sounds can you hear right now? Just listen. Don't judge the sounds like, *What an annoying drilling sound!*, just hear them. Do this for two or three minutes. Just like listening to your breath, this exercise takes you out of your thoughts and into witnessing the present moment. If you get bored of listening it means you're not being present and your mind is judging the activity.

How many times will you sit and listen to the sounds around you today? How can you make this a daily practice?

## Seeing is steering

You can also practice presence during habitual activities – like brushing your teeth or making tea – when your mind goes into default mode. In default mode, your actions become unconscious; this is the time when you put the milk in the cupboard and salt in the fridge. Use these habitual activities as a trigger to get present, an opportunity to rest your mind and feel alive.

By instructing your mind to notice new things, you steer your attention back to the present moment. Here's how to trigger the action:

*When I _____, what five new things can I notice?*

Pick one habitual daily activity. Next, create your trigger sentence. For example:

*When I walk to the station, what five new things can I notice?*

*When I make my coffee, what five new things can I notice?*

*When I sit at my desk, what five new things can I notice?*

## Taking the steering wheel

A week after roleplaying cold calls, Peter knew what to say and how to say it in his own way. One Monday afternoon he called.

> **Peter:** Anis, I feel worse. Now that I know what I should be saying, I feel more pressure and can't get the words out.
> **Anis:** What happened?
> **Peter:** I was supposed to make calls today, I tried to make a few, but I fumbled and started pitching.
> **Anis:** Why?

**Peter:** I was nervous.

**Anis:** Why?

**Peter:** Because I now know what I should be saying and that I was doing it all wrong before, so it felt more…pressured?

**Anis:** What's behind that pressure? What were you thinking?

**Peter:** I've got this list of 30 contacts to call, and I'm thinking if I mess up, there's only a finite number of prospects to call. If I mess this up, then I won't have a business.

**Anis:** Where are you right now?

**Peter:** In a breakout room.

**Anis:** What do you see around you?

**Peter:** Three walls...a glass wall...a monitor on the wall...

**Anis:** What can you hear, other than me?

**Peter:** I can hear some people talking outside. And the air conditioner.

**Anis:** What do you have to do right now?

**Peter:** What do you mean?

**Anis:** You've got a list of names and numbers in front of you. As soon as we finish our call, what do you have to do?

**Peter:** You mean call?

**Anis:** Yes, what do you have to do to call?

**Peter:** Dial the number…

**Anis:** Yes, so notice where you are and dial the number. Then what do you do?

**Peter:** I speak. Wait. I feel better. What happened?

**Anis:** Peter, thinking about your past mistakes and feeling concerned about your future stressed you out, which is why you couldn't remember what to say and why you froze. It's your body's fear response. To feel better, all you did was pay attention to where you are right now, instead of the past and future.

Peter went on to have a productive Tuesday making calls. He

wasn't as polished as a seasoned professional, but he had the power to overcome his previous limits, to practice and progress.

## More resources

In my humble view, Eckhart Tolle's book, *A New Earth: Awakening to Your Life's Purpose* is one of the best books on the topic of achieving mindful states.

## Be the watcher

Your focus determines your experience. It doesn't matter where you are physically, it's where you are mentally that matters. Whether you're in a tense meeting or relaxing with loved ones, if you're thinking about a proposal you must prepare, then you're not in that meeting or with your loved ones; you're sitting in front of your laptop, staring at that proposal.

Fear-infected action serves the ego's self-preservation agenda, which typically involves bringing others down. Solutions for collective positive outcomes won't arrive when your mind is occupied with the self. When the dark clouds of stress descend, collapse time by silencing your mind to embody your natural state of wonder. Stop getting caught up *in* your thoughts by *making space to watch* your thoughts.

# PRINCIPLE II

# Impose Your Intention

*The germ of defeat is in every selfish thought.*
- Charles F. Haanel, author and entrepreneur

*How people treat you is their karma; how you react is yours.*
- Wayne Dyer, author

*Playing with water, wet. Playing with fire, burned.*
- Indonesian proverb

Santos, a small business owner of a creative firm, and I sat down for a coffee one day. He opened his notebook on the table and mapped out his potential prospects, going through each one for me.

**Santos:** This prospect has lots of money, I am wondering how I can I work on this relationship... I only have a 30% chance of closing this other one, so it's not worth my time...this one here has a new business and I think maybe there's a 45% chance of increasing the revenue they give us...this one, I met them the other day and I want to know how I can speed up the process to close faster, they could be a good long-term regular client...and this one, they just want a website, but I want them to do video too so that should double the revenue I can get from them. So how do I move all these prospects down the pipeline faster, to turn them into money?

**Anis:** What do you know about these people?

**Santos:** What do you mean?

**Anis:** What do you know about them personally - their hopes, their dreams, their ambitions?

**Santos:** Nothing. Why? Does that matter?

**Anis:** Focus on getting to know them. Learn about their lives outside of work. Learn about their family. What's their favourite meal? Forget about trying to close them.

**Santos:** Okay, so I shouldn't just talk about business with them?

**Anis:** Get to know them as a person, understand what they're looking for, explore how you can help them. This takes your focus away from wondering how much money you can make from them. They can feel your energy and motives, from the questions you ask, the urgency in your voice, the quickness of your movement. It creates unconscious distrust in you. When you think someone is trying to take something from you, how does it make you, feel?

**Santos:** It makes me suspicious.

**Anis:** Would you talk to that person about your vulnerabilities?

**Santos:** Definitely not.

**Anis:** Why not?

**Santos:** I see your point. So I should stop selling to people. Instead, make friends is what you're saying?

**Anis:** Make friends, I love it! That's the spirit.

A week later we met for another session and this is what Santos had to say: "Anis, you taught me magic! Usually when I network, no one gives me their business card. This past week everyone gave me their business card. And when I met this client for dinner, he started telling me all sorts of stories about him, it was amazing!"

# The Danger Zone of Selling

If your motives are self-centred when meeting people – *How much can I get from this person? How can I nail this person as a client?* – you apply negative pressure on yourself because you're concerned about winning instead of being in the moment. The pressure of winning sets off the Hammer. An over-active Hammer clogs up the Coach's functions. Your fear-centred thoughts instruct your nervous system to emit negative body language, which the other person registers subconsciously.

Energetically, your fear-based thinking makes you vibrate at lower frequencies, repelling the people you can help and attracting people you'd rather not. When your focus is on closing the deal, your actions and behaviour reflect that intention. People can sniff selfishness and desperation a mile away; it's not a nice feeling being on the receiving end of ulterior motives.

*Law of the land*

*If we participate in the cause, it is not possible for us not to participate in the effect.*

– Gary Zukov

Understanding the law of cause and effect can really help you shift gears. You already know all your actions have consequences; Newton said so and the world agrees. It's called the law of motion:

*Every action has an equal and opposite reaction.*

– Isaac Newton

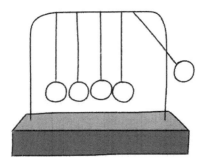

These metaphysical laws work the same for everyone, they don't pick favourites. If you throw me and her majesty the Queen of England into the Thames, we'll both fall into the river. One of us won't magically remain suspended in mid-air because one wears a crown and the other doesn't. It doesn't matter who you are, whatever energy you put out there is coming back to you and it all starts with your intention.

You need to ask yourself, "What energy am I putting out there?" When you give negativity to the world, you find negativity everywhere you turn. When you emit higher frequencies of love and kindness, or focus on people's strengths and virtues, you attract like forces, people and circumstances.

*You create your reality with your intentions.*

- Gary Zukov

## Shift from selling to serving

If you let your mind have its way, it will be influenced by constant environmental fear priming, triggering the Hammer, so your actions and behaviours will become self-serving. Instead, you need to take control and impose your intention.

The remedy to being ego-driven is shifting your intention from selling to serving. When you stop focusing on commission, cash flow and closing, you reduce the pressure of desperation and clear space in your head. Clearing the "clutter" of scarcity makes space for abundance to flow. You become a magnet, attracting higher frequency people and opportunities to you.

But it's not as easy as it sounds. You still need to make sales, or you'll have to update your CV and return to the daily grind of someone else's master plan. The desperation in people's voices is noticeable. Through gritted teeth they ask, "But how do you make them say yes, faster?" Stop trying to make them say yes, faster, and start finding ways to add value for them. Adding value gets them saying smaller yesses. Small yesses lead to that big yes.

When you shift your intention from selling to serving, you live consciously instead of paddling around unconsciously. You become the cause instead of an effect.

## Changing direction

Chinese diving athlete Yutong Luo failed to qualify to represent China for twelve years. A highly competitive athlete, he never made the cut. When it came to crunch time, his anxiety and stress sabotaged his performance despite receiving training around understanding the source of stress and changing belief patterns. Yet after participating in mindfulness-based training, Yutong won his first gold medal at London's Olympic Games in August 2012.

So what happened? Before mindfulness training, Luo was absolutely obsessed with winning gold and this obsession weakened his performance. Being ego-driven, like desperately trying to close a deal or land your job, leaves you easily threatened, which triggers your Hammer. Luo didn't know how to deal with the overwhelming emotions derived from the threats, like competing athletes or his own variable performances. After mindfulness training, he shifted from trying to control his anxieties, to separating himself from them. He also changed his goal from winning to a values-driven approach; instead of trying to get the gold, he focused on realising his maximum potential.

When your sense of self-worth depends on you winning and others losing, the result is that you feel powerless, not powerful. Instead of being driven by the desire to win, focus on making a positive difference in the lives of others. If you're not single-mindedly focused on serving them and honouring the moment, your mind is partly thinking of the self. When you are lead by the ego, you prevent yourself from reaching peak flow states, where the doing and the being is the end in itself, as opposed to a means to the end. When you honour the moment and respect the work performed in each breath, that's where you perform at your best. You develop deep satisfaction in executing your craft.

In his book, *Pour Your Heart Into It*, former Starbucks CEO Howard Schultz talked about the importance of values very early in Starbucks' journey. It was important for him to be clear about what Starbucks stood for because you end up communicating your values with your every action and every decision. Are you focused on making more money or making more people successful?

### *The priceless gift of understanding*

One client I worked with, Aneesha, left the high-octane environment of investment banking to work for herself as a consultant helping people with their investments. After a few coaching sessions she realised that when she met people she would ask herself, "How can I win this client?" She didn't like that feeling. The focus on taking was not aligned with who she was and how she wanted to grow her business.

After changing her intention from *How will I win this client?* to *How can I help this person?* she replaced a focus on her spiel with *Let me listen and give them the gift of understanding.* Shortly after, a prospective client said, "I felt like you really listened to me." She eventually signed that client. How often do people say that to you?

## High no, high yes

Early on in my new chapter as a speaker and workshop leader, I was called last minute by the founder of a company to run a masterclass for his clients. They could not meet my fee but to compensate, they promised loads of promotion and activities that would be great for a fledgling business. I explained the logic behind my fee and accepted the lower fee on the condition they fulfil the promise of promotional activities. They were happy with the session and the workshop feedback from participants was the best they had ever received, so I was happy.

Nine months later, the CEO contacted me to run another masterclass. In my reply, I reminded him of my fee and explained that whilst I didn't expect him to match that fee, I hoped we could meet in the middle. His reply was angry. He accused me of being unethical because I was charging high prices. He used moral superiority to tread on my value. I was shocked and angered by his response.

After breathing and centring myself, I remembered that psychologists called his communication a classic case of *projecting*, where deep unconscious feelings of personal shortcomings are projected onto others. *He's insecure about something. He doesn't mean to harm me.*

I called him. His tone was defensive and stern, but he calmed down after realising he hadn't read my email to the end where I suggested a middle ground. He flatly refused to negotiate fees, promising he'd promote me in all the other ways he'd promised before. I said, "I appreciate the gesture, Ryan, but that's what you said last time and nothing happened. Since you were happy with the workshop – you said it yourself, it was the best feedback you'd received – and if you'd like your next customers to gain hope, confidence and core skills to thrive so you can make your programme a success, isn't it fair to meet in the middle?"

He later emailed me insisting on the same low fee. Before replying, I sent him thoughts of loving kindness, wishing him and his company well. I immersed myself in my purpose. I reminded myself why I was doing all of this, why charging more and getting paid more was for the greater good. So I could ultimately reach and serve more people.

Then I sent my reply: "Appreciate your consideration, if you can't find anyone, you know where I am."

Two hours later I received a call from someone who attended a talk I ran elsewhere, asking me to train his team. He didn't bat an eye at my fee.

## Forks and Frequencies

There will be times when you have to say no. Sometimes it's the wrong prospect or the offer is too low. It's annoying if they insist upon a lower fee, making you shift your flow and grudgingly saying no. I call this a "low no", a rejection that comes from a negative place. And as you send out a wave of negativity, you can expect that same energy to meet you, as sure as Newton's laws of motion.

There is a famous physics demonstration that involves two tuning forks tuned to the same frequency. Striking the first tuning fork against a hard surface causes the second tuning fork to resonate, i.e. to hum at the same pitch, even though you haven't touched the second fork.

*What frequency are you attracting?*

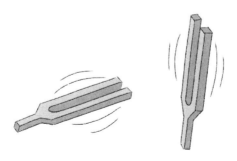

Striking the first fork causes it to vibrate, forcing the surrounding air particles into vibrational motion. The vibrating air particles force the second tuning fork, which is of the same frequency as the first one, into vibrational motion. If there were a third tuning fork of a different frequency, it would not vibrate.

Just like that second untouched tuning fork, people vibrating at the same frequency resonate with the energy you emit. If you're operating at lower frequencies, you attract prospects who want to stamp down your fees and people who don't value your services. Refusing opportunities when you feel resentful radiates bitterness. To prevent negative events and people boomeranging back to you, elevate your frequency and give a "high no" or a "high yes", by imposing your intention.

To help you impose your intention for how you want to show up in business and life, fill in the blank and answer the questions of the frequency tuner below.

## Frequency Tuner Technique

*I want people's first impression of me to be…*

*Three things I can do to create this impression are…*
Instead of specific actions like making eye contact, firm handshake or repeating their name, focus on states of being like being deeply curious about the other person.

*The best version of me would show up on my best day…*

*Who do I deeply respect, and what three qualities in that person do I admire?*

*Three things I can do to embody these characteristics are…*

## Scrap scripted plays

Your energy and motives are sensed by others, even when you're hiding behind the veil of tinned techniques and scripted plays. Real communication between people is not verbal; words are just tools of the mind, building blocks of the ego. To make an impact, you need to communicate on the level of the spirit, the oneness that connects us all. To connect with their soul, it's not what you say that matters, but how you feel and what you do. Affection must be expressed through action. When you intensely experience love, joy and the willingness to serve people, you radiate trust and abundance. People will feel that.

Rather than following scripted playbooks, commanding how you'll *be,* instead of letting fear seep in, allows your natural approach to flower. It's the difference between acting and being sincere.

*When you're serving instead of selling, you will be compelling.*

# PRINCIPLE III

# Notice the Good

*Remember that what you now have was once among the things you only hoped for.*
*- Epicurus, Greek philosopher*

*When you are grateful, fear disappears, abundance appears.*
*- Tony Robbins, business and life strategist*

*If you aren't grateful for what you already have, what makes you think you would be happy with more?*
*- Roy T Bennett, author and philosopher*

**M**akena, a brilliant and passionate sustainable development consultant, started her own company after many years working for someone else. As an employee, she was regularly assigned projects so she never had to find work; there was a dedicated team who did that.

In her first year of self-employment, work came easy, through referrals. She secured a nice portfolio of medium and long-term contracts. Life was good. But a year later, after the long-term projects dried up, Makena's next quarter prospects and revenue looked discomfortingly thin. During that initial year of "easy work" gained through referrals, she neglected to market herself.

Her joy increasingly gave way to an undercurrent of dread and despair that obstructed her from being proactive and effective. It started eating away at her confidence even though Makena was a confident orator, prolific writer and highly regarded in her industry. The thing with confidence is that when you lose it in one specific part of your life it contaminates other areas. The reverse is also true; when you grow wings of confidence in one area, it lifts you up in other ways.

## Ignorance is Not Bliss

When you work for yourself, you prefer doing the bits you love and the bits you're good at; these bits usually coincide with the primary reason clients pay you. But you avoid doing the bits you hate and that bring you stress, like selling yourself. It's human nature and it's called procrastination. As an executive and industry expert, you may feel selling is beneath your dignity or that you are far too qualified to sell. It's also quite daunting when you've never done it before, especially if you're carrying negative baggage around this activity called "selling". Desperation creeps in about how you're going to make this self-employed thing work. The thought of giving up your freedom to become someone else's employee is about as enticing as a hangman's noose.

Working with Makena, we first had to alleviate this general feeling of discomfort and help elevate her energy. It's hard to see the good when you constantly see and feel the bad. I invited Makena to start a daily gratitude journal in which she wrote three things she was grateful for that day and why.

Ten days after beginning her daily journaling, Makena said she felt more positive and that the exercise brought about more constructive events. The "right" type of people started flowing into her life. She had engaging and constructive conversations with more frequency, paving the path to new proposals and projects. Let's look at the science behind why this works.

## Your personal bouncer

We are bombarded with millions of messages a day and to protect us from information overwhelm, the brain employs a bouncer called the Reticular Activating System. The Bouncer determines what information is allowed in and directs your brain to relevant information, opportunities and resources, depending on where your attention is.

The other day my wife and I went to our friend's house for dinner. Using my smartphone, I mapped directions from our home to our friend's address. There was a tonne of information staring back at me on the screen – hundreds of roads, thousands of buildings, infinite paths – but Google Maps highlighted my route with a single blue line. Your Bouncer works in a similar manner, sifting through millions of bits of information, highlighting what's in the realm of your subconscious attention.

See for yourself. Close your eyes and say "blue" ten times. Then open your eyes and look around the room. What do you see? Try the exercise again, only this time say the word "red" ten times. If you instructed yourself properly, everything blue and red in the room would have jumped to the forefront of your attention.

This little science experiment demonstrates how your Bouncer works; seek and you will find. The trouble is, most of the time our mind's default mode instructs us to focus on the negative.

## Taming Your Negative Bias

In a 3-week gratitude study published by the *Journal of Personality and Social Psychology*[8], participants were split into three groups. Researchers instructed group A to journal daily about things that annoyed them, group B to write daily gratitude exercises and group C, the control group, to write whatever they wanted to about their day in their journals. In addition, at the end of each day, participants had to submit a life satisfaction survey on subjective well-being and health behaviours, like how long they slept, how easy it was to sleep, whether they exercised and changes to their outlook on life. These daily exercises took about five minutes to complete. Researchers also asked the participant's spouse or significant other to fill out a questionnaire on their observations of their partner's well-being.

After three weeks, participants from group B said they were considerably more satisfied with their lives than at the beginning of the experiment. They also felt more optimistic about the coming week, felt more connected to others, slept more and spent more time vigorously exercising than participants in the control group. They also reported a higher incidence of helping others.

Furthermore, two types of gratitude exercises were tested: daily and weekly journaling. Daily gratitude journaling was significantly more powerful than weekly journaling in achieving positive outcomes.

This study shows that investing time daily to contemplate what's good in your life sets you up for success. Think of it as *investing* instead of *spending* time; like all good investments, you get back much more than you put in.

Appreciation is the antidote to arrogance, a remedy for rejection and a solution for suffering. You can't feel pride and gratitude at once. You can't feel appreciation and anger or humiliation at the same time. Nor can you feel fear and grace together. And remember, after just 90 seconds you have a choice over what you think. Will you let the fictitious thoughts fester, or will you plant new seeds in the soil of your mind and allow new empowered thoughts to flower? As long as you decide to let venomous thoughts linger, you let yourself, your business, your colleagues and your family down.

*A person who feels entitled to everything will be grateful for nothing. Gratitude is the antidote to entitlement.*

— Robert Emmons

## Denial, Delusion, Decisions

You might be asking yourself, "Aren't I denying my emotions by trying to eliminate them or sugar-coat them with gratitude?" Not at all. I'm not suggesting you deny your emotions or bottle them up. Absolutely feel them. Accept and acknowledge them. Just don't linger in them, otherwise your emotions will control you. When you let the Hammer rule, it leads to impulsive, reactionary behaviours. Your life becomes a stream of unconscious effects instead of a result of conscious decisions.

Maybe you're wondering, "Would feeling appreciation make me careless and demotivated?" If you're concerned that feeling *too* grateful undermines your motivation, let's take a moment to consider what motivates us.

## What moves you

When it comes to motivation, self-determination theory states that we have three universal needs to satisfy[9] in order to be happy, content and motivated: competence, or your ability to learn skills and do a job well; autonomy, or your "power" to choose; and connection, because we all have an innate desire to feel like we're a part of something, a community or a shared cause. Satisfying these needs is critical avoid behaving like a jerk or becoming depressed.

Without meeting these three universal needs, you become easily bored and disengaged. You'd rather sit on the sofa and binge-watch Netflix and gorge on junk food. This may sound appealing, but research shows that being a lazy bum does not make us feel good.

Now that you know your three core psychological needs around motivation, let's consider the two major sources of drive so you know how to motivate yourself and others. An external drive is satisfied by external rewards such as praise, social approval or money and other material goods. People that are externally driven do not necessarily enjoy what they're doing, but do the thing anyway for the payoff. Examples include a tennis player who plays for endorsements and trophies or a salesperson who hates selling but craves the above-average salary.

Internally motivated people do things for the joy of it; they seek novelty and love to challenge themselves. An internally motivated tennis player plays for the love of the game and the challenge of cultivating the perfect ace. An internally motivated salesperson sells because they love meeting people and relish the challenge of figuring out how to help clients overcome their problems.

Studies show internally motivated people are more confident, interested and excited than externally motivated people. This manifests in better performance, persistence, creativity and enhanced well-being, regardless of your level of competence.

You must nurture your inner force because it's easily stifled by unsupportive external forces such as the media, negative people, toxic environments or unconscious bosses. Furthermore, rewards or punishment that depend on your performance of tasks significantly undermines intrinsic motivation [10]. In my corporate sales role my motivation was constantly derailed by external pressures. I had to constantly cultivate my internal motivation by reminding myself of the joy of meeting people and helping them overcome their challenges.

Remember, constantly connect with your why.

## Isn't gratitude demotivating?

Feeling appreciative does not undermine your motivation, but rather enhances it by protecting you from the pervasive pull of external forces contaminating your beliefs and attention. Daily experiences of failure, rejection and comparison undermine your confidence. Your perceived self-worth and value underpin your motivation[11]. Comparing your progress with others deflates your self-worth faster than a balloon zips around the room, taking your motivation with it.

Like a toddler, your natural state is one of joy, curiosity, adventure and growth, but culture, consumerism and the wheels of capitalism suck it out of you. Feeling appreciative is your protective shield from the external messages telling you to do and be more because you're less or unworthy if you don't. Feeling appreciation gives you space to cultivate your intrinsic motivation, where you are enough, where you do and be more for the sheer joy of experiencing how far and how fast you can go to become all you can be.

### Isn't gratitude a catch-22?

Isn't gratitude a catch-22, meaning, you need things to be grateful for before you can be grateful? Are you telling me that you have absolutely nothing to be grateful for right now? Did you have to create the internet or build paved pathways to walk on or pay for the heart keeping you alive? When you shift your perspective and stop taking things for granted there's always something to be grateful for.

Just like a car parked in a space prevents another car from parking there, a mind occupied with appreciation blocks out toxic thoughts. If I tell you right now, "Stop thinking about that awful meeting. Stop thinking about it or you'll feel worse," you'll keep thinking about it because you're inadvertently being directed there. It's the way your brain works. Instead I could ask, "Tell me about that fab meeting you had with a prospect. How did it go? What was good about it?" These questions guide you toward constructive thoughts and ideas, steering you out of the choppy waters of anxiety.

## Taking the Reins

Allowing a poisonous thought to fester in your head is like inviting a mob of angry drunk hooligans to your house party – things can get ugly, fast. Negative thoughts attract more negative thoughts and before you know it, you've bought a one-way ticket to Depressionville. Consciously cultivating appreciation helps elevate you to higher emotional and empowered states. When you operate from empowered states, you silence the Hammer and awaken the Coach. From a powerful state you let the flow of insight and inspiration meet you. You vibrate at higher frequencies.

Do you remember the last time you were served by someone who hated their job or just didn't want to be there? It's not nice, is it? On the other hand, joyful people are fun to be around; their presence is infectious, lifting the mood of the people around them.

## Putting appreciation into practice

Use these questions to guide your daily practice and steer you in times of stress:

*What am I grateful for?*
Answer by saying what you're grateful for and why. List at least one personal and professional qualities about yourself.

*What do I enjoy?*
For three minutes, list all the things you like and enjoy.

*Who are three people I can send a thank you note to right now?*
Go ahead and send that thank you note; brighten not only your day but theirs.

The more positive energy you put out there, the more you get in return. Here's another technique I call the Floodlight; it's a great one to practice while you're waiting for something or commuting.

*Bring three people to mind you'd like to thank.*

*Next, imagine you're pointing a floodlight of gratitude at them, one by one.*

Keeping a gratitude journal and making it a daily practice to write three things you're grateful for (and why) has helped one of my clients create new leads by inspiring her to try a new lead generation strategy that she hadn't thought of before. The daily practice trains your brain to look out for opportunities because in the absence of bad, all the good appears. Be careful though; when writing about what you are grateful for, make sure your source of gratitude is not a comparison to other people. Avoid statements like *I'm so grateful I'm better looking than Sandra* or *I'm so grateful I'm the only one I know with a PhD*. Comparisons elicit toxic emotions like pride and envy, leaving you operating at lower states and vulnerable to the vortex of anxiety and depression.

## Celebrating you

It can be difficult to see the good when you're constantly reminded of all that is bad. The brain's negativity bias tricks you into feeling heightened states of fear, which prevent you from creating your best work. But appreciation redirects and rewires your brain to look for the good around you. You'll never not think about negative things, but the more you practice focusing on blessings instead of burdens, the more you notice blessings. It becomes a virtuous cycle.

The turning point for former world champion triathlete Siri Lindley occurred when her motivation shifted. Competing became less about winning and more about using her talent and abilities to their fullest, a mode of celebrating and demonstrating her appreciation of her gifts and skills.

How can you use all that you possess – your ability, character, determination, passion, desire – to help others? How can you use these things to their fullest potential, as a celebration of you?

# PRINCIPLE IV

# Don't Assume

*Illusions mistaken for truth are the pavement under our feet.*
- Barbara Kingsolver, author

*An unquestioned mind is the world of suffering.*
- Byron Katie, author

*Your assumptions are your windows on the world, scrub them off every once in a while, or the light won't come in.*
- Isaac Asimov, writer and professor

During client meetings with colleagues, Anjali's strategy was to make herself invisible. Observing meetings instead of participating was safer – if she didn't say anything, she could do no wrong. When her boss said, "You were quiet in there," she'd respond, "I was listening." This statement is only half true. She listened, but her silence disguised a deathly fear of saying something stupid, revealing the imposter she believed she was.

Before meetings, Anjali's stomach engaged in international knotting contests, forcing her to lose hours of productive time. She ruminated over concerns of her stupidity materialising in meetings and all the consequences of appearing dumb and how she'd lose her job and never get hired again. Yes, Anjali was listening, but instead of hearing the conversation in the room, she focused on the conversation in her head.

This mental ordeal plays out like clockwork before, during and after every client or internal meeting. Worse still, during internal meetings Anjali's strategy was *offence is the best defence*. Since she was offensively defensive all the time, i.e. snapping back at any perceived criticism, it was difficult for colleagues to have constructive conversations with her. Internal meetings with her felt like rugby scrums of pulling and pushing, rather than passing the ball to a teammate to take it over the finish line.

In our coaching session I asked Anjali about her behaviour.

Anis: Before yesterday's meeting with your boss, what were you assuming?

Anjali: I assumed I'd say something wrong. What if I don't know the answer, then I'll appear stupid and I haven't done the work.

Anis: But is that true?

Anjali: Is what true?

Anis: That you haven't done the work?

Anjali: No. I always do the work.

Anis: Even if you didn't know the answer, does that mean you're stupid?

Anjali: No.

Anis: How is making those assumptions, that you might say something wrong, that you might get caught out, affecting you?

Anjali: It's really really stressful. I never look forward to meetings and I'm always on edge.

## The Silent Killer

When someone makes a face and talks in a certain tone, how often do you make up a story as to why they're making that face or speaking in that tone, a story that has something to do with you, which affects your response to them? They then react to your reaction and a misunderstanding ensues.

Making assumptions paralyses your productivity and creates avoidable stress. There is a way to stop the assumptions in its tracks. Asking questions clears the flood of assumptions flooding your psyche. Instead of letting assumptions cascade through your mind, be courageous and ask questions until you're clear and even then, don't assume you know all there is to know about a situation.

Next time you find yourself getting stressed or upset about something or someone, ask yourself, "What assumption am I making here? What do I know for sure?" When you have established you don't know the facts, decide to shelve the issue until you can ask for clarification from the person involved. You can always worry about it later when you know the facts.

Of course, it's not as easy at is sounds. When your mind courses along the negative railway tracks, it likes to take the long scenic route. Remember your mind's default modes, the Sports Commentator and Me Me Me? Let's take a deeper look at how they get you into all sorts of trouble, and what you can do about it.

## Constant Commentary

The table 1 on the next page outlines the common types of commentary your mind plays out. This is the categorisation used by Judith Beck[12], one of the world's authorities on Cognitive Behavioural Therapy, but I have tried to simplify the language to offset some of the jargon.

*Table 1. Common types of commentary*

| Commentary blunders | What it is | How it sounds in your head |
|---|---|---|
| *Polarised thinking* | Viewing situations or circumstances only in two absolute categories | If I'm not a total success, I'm a complete failure. |
| *Misfortune-telling* | Predicting the future is all doom and gloom and there can't possibly be any other likely outcome. | It won't arrive on time, then we'll miss the deadline and won't get a refund. |
| *Subtracting the positive* | Irrationally discount and subtract positive occurrences and focus on the negative | I was just lucky; that doesn't count; that's not much. |
| *Sweeping statements* | Generalised negative conclusions that imply ramifications last forever | I felt uncomfortable in the meeting, I don't have what it takes to sell, ever |
| *All about me* | Believing others behave negatively because of you, without considering plausible explanations for their behaviour | My client was short with me because I said or did something wrong. |
| *Feelings as truth* | Relying on feelings to prove something is true, ignoring any factual evidence that proves it's untrue | He said it's okay, but I still feel like I've done something wrong. |
| *Magnify & miniaturise* | Arbitrarily magnifying the negative and/or miniaturising the positive in yourself, people or situations. | Losing that sale proves I'm rubbish at sales. Securing that contract doesn't mean I can sell. |
| *Reality distortion* | Paying disproportionate attention to one tiny negative aspect while excluding the bigger picture. | I received one 3-star rating (and 7 5-star ratings), so my workshop was awful. |

The emotional and physical manifestations of these thoughts cause significant distress, which can last for hours, days or even weeks. But it can all be avoided.

When you're triggered by a stimulus, such as an email or something someone said, you experience a reflexive emotional reaction that causes your brain to release stress chemicals. The chemical released by your brain creates a physiological experience. Remember the 90-second rule? When you're triggered, the stress subsides after 90 seconds. If you continue feeling stressed after those initial 90 seconds, it is out of choice. But here's the catch, it's only a choice if you're aware of this trigger. Without awareness, the stress takes over. Now that you know this mechanism, you have a choice.

Making the choice to change the direction of your thoughts is not as easy as it sounds. You have to catch the thought early and to do this you need to be aware of your thoughts, without judging or explaining them. On table 2 are some strategies to direct your attention:

*Table 2. Commentator coping strategies*

| Commentary blunders | How it sounds | Strategy |
|---|---|---|
| *Polarised thinking* | If I'm not a total success, I'm a complete failure. | What would I tell my best friend if they were in the same position? |
| *Misfortune-telling* | By sacking him, he will hate me and I'll ruin his life. This is going to be horrendous. | Is this 100% true? How often have you worried in the past, where things never turn out as bad as you thought? |
| *Subtracting the positive* | I was just lucky; that doesn't count; that's not much. | What evidence supports this idea? What's the evidence against this idea? |
| *Sweeping statements* | I messed up that meeting, I don't have what it takes. | What would you tell your best friend? |
| *All about me* | My client was short with me because I said/did something wrong. | What alternative explanation can you think of for your client's behaviour? |
| *Feelings as truth* | He said it's okay, but I still feel like I've done something wrong. | What's the worst that could happen? (Follow-up question) What's the best that could happen? |
| *Magnify & miniaturise* | Losing that sale proves I'm crap. Securing that contract doesn't mean I can sell. | What evidence supports the idea? Evidence against? |
| *Reality distortion* | My workshop was terrible. I received a 3-star rating (and 7 5-star ratings). | Evidence supporting idea? Evidence against? |

To get started using one of these strategies, it helps to create a

"What Am I Thinking" record, which requires you to simply list what your constant commentator says. After listing your thoughts, evaluate your constant commentator using one of the strategies in the right-hand column from the table above.

*(For more coping strategies, download your "What Am I Thinking?" worksheet at http://anisqizilbash.com/book-resources/)*

## The 90/10 Rule

Sometimes the constant commentator is right. For example, you miss a deadline, or you are late for a meeting. It's a fact, there's no reality distortion. But focussing on missing the deadline won't make you feel better, nor will it help you come up with a solution. If your car's wheel gets stuck in the mud, pointing and screaming won't get you out of your sticky situation.

Instead, focus 90% of your attention and energy on finding and executing a solution. When the mind gets moving, it's difficult to stop. Imagine for a moment your car is tearing down the motorway at 100 mph and you're about to collide head-on with a lorry. Slamming on the breaks won't save you but changing lanes might. You don't have to stop your thoughts, just give them a detour.

Here are a few questions to ask yourself that helped my clients out of sticky situations:

*When you are overwhelmed with tasks, ask yourself, "What can I do right now to improve the situation?"*

*When a thought or situation causes you incredible stress, ask yourself, "What's good about these circumstances?"*

*When faced with a problem, ask yourself, "What's the opportunity waiting to be expressed?"*

*When you're about to do something you have to do instead of something you want to do, ask yourself, "How can I make this fun?"*

When the situation arises, keep asking yourself the question until you come up with at least one or two ideas. When you do, you set new thought energy in motion, propelling you to feel a new emotion.

*Every adversity brings with it the seed of an equivalent advantage.*

– Napoleon Hill

## Common assumptions

Jing received an invite to an event from an influential person. Assuming she was mistakenly emailed, she planned to ignore the message. She considered calling to clarify. Her first instinct was to doubt herself. "What if they're busy and get annoyed with my call? What if it was a mistake and I wasn't supposed to receive the invite?" Then she asked herself, "What am I assuming? I don't know anything for sure. Forget it, I'm just going to call." It turns out the email was intended for her and she was encouraged to attend. If Jing had listened to her mind's constant commentary, she would have ignored the email and missed an opportunity to meet investors.

Awareness of how your assumptions obstructs your progress gives you the power to stop them, because you can't stop what you can't see. Here are other common assumptions and how they hinder your success:

*You think the person you are calling will hate your call or hate you.*

This typically stops you from calling.

*You think you detect a tone in their voice or they laugh and you assume they're thinking ill of you.*

Assuming others think ill of you changes what you say. You're likely to be defensive or offensive.

*Your mind goes into sci-fi story-telling mode as you (mis)interpret the tone or language of an email.*

Your interpretation changes your communication.

*You assume others have the same technical or market knowledge as you.*

They don't understand what you're saying and they're too embarrassed to admit it, so they stay silent and then never call you back.

*You think you know what the other person wants, thinks and feels.*

Doing this stops you from asking how they feel, leaving the other person feeling misunderstood and unheard.

*You interpret someone with crossed arms crossed and a scrunched-up face as bored or judgmental.*

You assume they're bored or think you're full of rubbish. They're about to ask a question that will reveal you for the fraud you are. Or maybe it's just their natural resting face. I can't tell you how many times this has happened to me when I first started public speaking.

What assumptions does your mind make? Notice how the illusions it weaves stop you from creating opportunities.

## Neutralise assumption

In all these examples, in all situations where you're assuming, you need to question yourself because you cannot influence others without first influencing yourself. If you're still under the spell of supposing, you will react reflexively instead of reflectively. If you're still under the enchantment of assuming, your reactions will be defensive, which can be perceived as offensive because the Hammer is triggered. You're acting from survival mode rather than from an enlightened mode

To remove the venom from your mind's assiduous assumptions, use the ALIGN technique:

**Assumption:** What am I assuming?
**Likelihood:** What's the likelihood this will actually happen?
**Is this useful:** If I'm not 100% certain it will happen, is this a good use of my time?
**Get clarity:** What can I ask to clear this up? And who can I ask?
**New information:** I will defer the issue until I speak to said person and get new information.

Assumptions close doors. Questions open doors.

*Remember your 90-second window*

Your mind spins Nobel-worthy stories, makes epic assumptions, triggering your Hammer. When you learn to question the dark shadows cast by assumptions, you will liberate yourself from the darkness of suffering. You have a 90-second window during which the effects of your automatic thought wear off. After 90 seconds, you get to decide, "Do I want to keep going down this route to darkness, or take a detour to the light of happiness?"

# PRINCIPLE V

# Free Yourself

*What you perceive in others, you strengthen in yourself*
- Dr. Helen Schucman, author of A Course In Miracles

*The ability to observe without evaluating is the highest form of intelligence.*
- Jiddu Krishnamurti, philosopher

*If you judge people, you have no time to love them.*
- Mother Teresa, Nobel Peace Prize Winner

One day I called a huge international media agency that looks after the account of a major technology company. None of my predecessors had ever cracked the technology account.

After successfully arranging a meeting with the account director over a brief call, I gazed out the window with squinted eyes and wondered why the meeting had been so easy to set up. When the day of the meeting rolled around, instead of reviewing my pitch or thinking about the meeting in reception, I practiced a new breathing technique to get present.

Kaito hurried in, greeted me with glazed eyes, shallow breaths and a furrowed brow. He shook my hand without making eye contact and directed me to the meeting area. After taking our seats, Kaito laid into me. "You salespeople make my life hell. People from your company are rude, arrogant and selfish and you just don't care about anyone but yourselves. Who the hell do you think you are calling up our clients and cutting out our commission? You don't tell us what's going on, you go straight to the client and that makes us look incompetent.

A volcano of anger roiled inside of me. *How dare he speak to me like this!* On the verge of standing up and spitting those words at him like venom, I took a breath, and observed the thought until it faded over the horizon of my mind. *He doesn't know you. He's right, our company has a reputation for being callous and cavalier. But we have never met before, so he couldn't possibly be talking about me.* These thoughts whizzed past my mind like a bullet train. As I focused on my breath, the thoughts vanished. Instead of judging him, I listened, letting his comments pass through me like the wind rustling through tree leaves.

Half a minute later, Kaito's energy shifted. It was as if he had broken out of a trance and suddenly he realized, with regret, what he had said.

Anis: I'm glad you got that off your chest. I don't blame you. Yes, the company has a bad rep for being aggressive. Is there anything else you want to discuss?
Kaito: Eh, no. I'm so sorry, I've had a week from hell and another call from your company put me over the edge, that's no way to speak to someone.
Anis: I'm sorry you've had to go through this. What would you like to see done differently?
Kaito: Just keep us in the loop.
Anis: Okay. Anything else?
Kaito: Don't talk price with our clients, leave that to us.
Anis: Okay. Is that all?
Kaito: I'd rather you didn't talk directly to our clients.
Anis: Kaito, clients don't belong to anyone and if I bump into them at events, I can't not talk to them. That would be rude.
Kaito: Fine.
Anis: Look, I get it, we leave you out of the loop so you look silly and you might lose the account. Right? Let's change that, by keeping in touch. I have an idea.

For the next fifteen minutes we tossed around some ideas to help our mutual client achieve their objective. Three months after our meeting, Kaito placed a £30,000 order with us. The following year he booked a further £50,000.

# The Fog of Emotion

Had I reacted to Kaito's outburst with aggression or anger, do you think he would have booked business with us? Unlikely. Had I stormed out, it's likely I would have lost an £80,000 opportunity. It's likely my afternoon would have been unproductive. It's likely I would have carried that anger home with me and been awful company for my wife and cat. You know what it's like when the dark clouds of anger descend – they hang around for a while and make everyone's life miserable.

Recognising the rising tide of judgement, I let it ebb away through observation. Instead of labelling him an insensitive jerk, I offered compassion. Instead of convicting him of eternal idiocy, I left space for understanding. And because I offered positive energy, soon enough, Kaito realized he was being unreasonable and his emotions eventually mirrored mine.

The fifth principle is to free yourself from judgement. They're doing the best they can. When you judge people, it affects what you say and how you act in their company. People often get nervous meeting "big-wig" clients. But judging others to be superior necessarily makes you feel inferior and therefore alerts your Hammer. I'm not suggesting you act entitled or disrespectful, but rather that you simply be present and be yourself. Self-doubt or pride are fear-centred feelings. You're not going to say anything authentic, creative or meaningful from fearful or prideful states.

Dale Carnegie summed it up best when he said, "Give the other person a fine reputation to live up to." When you see the best in people, they will surprise you and rise to what you see in them. Cognitive science and psychology call this phenomenon *confirmation bias*, which is the brain's tendency to search for evidence, prioritise information and interpret facts to confirm one's own belief systems. We all like to believe we are good and well-meaning individuals. Furthermore, when focused on your internal commentator's judgement, you're not listening to others. Next time you find yourself in the company of others, watch yourself judging them. What labels are you sticking on them? Observing what you think creates a gap for you to let the labels fall away, leaving space to listen.

## Covered in Sticky Labels

Another form of judgement stifling your flow is self-judgement. What do you say to yourself when you mess up or try something new? Self-judgement leads to self-doubt and a lack of self-belief. When thoughts like *what if I can't do this, why would anyone listen to me, who am I to say or do this* are allowed to fester, the Hammer erects a wall of fear and doubt, stopping you from taking action. Before you know it, you're squirming on the floor covered with Post-it Notes of labels you stuck on yourself.

*Labels you stuck on yourself*

Famed cognitive psychologist on self-motivation Albert Bandura claims your perceived confidence in your ability influences the behaviours you choose, your expectations, how much effort you put in and how much you persevere in the face of obstacles. Eliminating defensive behaviour such as making excuses or blaming others is also important to help you push through barriers.

Stanford Professor of Psychology Carol Dweck is known for her work on mindset. In her best-selling book, *Mindset: Changing the Way You Think to Fulfil Your Potential*[13] she reveals,

The view you adopt for yourself profoundly affects the way you lead your life. It can determine whether you become the person you want to be and whether you accomplish the things you value.

## Talent is overrated

Dweck claims we have two modes of mindset – a fixed and a growth mindset. If you have a *fixed mindset,* you believe you have a certain amount of innate intelligence and ability. Your potential is carved in stone and there's no possibility of improving. You're driven by the desire to prove yourself over and over again. Then there's the *growth mindset,* where you believe the hand you're dealt is just the starting point and you can develop from there. You believe you can cultivate more qualities and skill through effort and everyone can change and grow through practice and experience.

A greater predictor of your success is not your talent or skills, but your self-belief. How much you believe in yourself determines how much effort you put in. How much you believe in yourself determines what you do today, whether it's picking up your tools to start creating a masterpiece to share with the world or snoozing, binge-watching Netflix and swiping through the social media feeds of other successful people.

The labels you stick on yourself stop you before anyone else can. You reject yourself before anyone gets the chance to witness your magic. Imagine, *what if?* What could you do if you were courageous and broke through your wall of fear? When an eagle faces a storm it flies higher. What if you used the punishing winds of adversity to soar to new heights? What if you took action, put yourself out there and started growing?

Beware the labels you stick on yourself. Start by writing them down, then ripping them up. They don't serve you on your journey.

*Self-belief does not necessarily ensure success, but self-disbelief assuredly spawns failure.*

- Albert Bandura

When you're trapped in a spiral of self-judgement, it's hard to believe in yourself. Those labels are thought habits stuck on repeat. The good news is you can change them. A belief is just a thought you think over and over again. To climb out of the spiral of disempowering thoughts and think new empowering thoughts, you have to click pause, download a new track and press play.

Use the BOLD technique below to snap out of spirals of self-judgement and reboot your self-belief.

## BOLD Technique

### Be aware

You can't change what you can't see, so the first step is to be aware of your mind's thought patterns. A good starting point is noticing how you're feeling. Where is stress manifesting in your body? Do you feel like a hippo is sitting on your chest? A fish flopping around in your stomach? A boa-constrictor around your neck? Write down how you're feeling, preferably using a pen and paper instead of an electronic device. It will help you focus.

### Overcome

Think back to an achievement you are proud of, a time where you overcame an obstacle or endured a challenge.

### Live it

Next, recall what you did to achieve the win, running it like a video in your mind. Recall a moment you felt like giving up but you kept going. Finally see yourself achieving it – where were you and what were you wearing? Embody the emotion. Maybe you smile or pump your fist but make a gesture or move your body as you would if you achieved it now.

### Declare appreciation & love

Now close your eyes and declare your love and appreciation to yourself for becoming the person you had to become to overcome the obstacle and achieve that goal. *That* person brought you to where you are now, and that same person will take you where you want to go. That person will help you, support you, show you how to achieve your goal. You did it before and you will do everything you can to do it again. Say thank you and feel the love.

Use the BOLD technique to give you a confidence boost before meetings and presentations or when you're feeling stressed or stuck.

# The Agony and Ecstasy of Alternative Facts

Rubina, a coaching client, was quite annoyed with herself one morning. "They said yes right away. If only I'd asked for more, I could have closed that new client for £3,800 instead of £3000! I can't believe I blew that chance." Her meeting – the one where she closed new business – occurred the day before, but that *if only* feeling cost her a day's productivity and a good night's sleep. Our brain has a remarkable way of making us feel awful even when we've done something great by our standards. Sometimes when we've won we feel like we've lost.

In a study published in the *Journal of Personality and Social Psychology*[14], researchers investigated levels of satisfaction of gold, silver and bronze medallists. One might think that their level of satisfaction would mirror their pecking order but the results proved otherwise. The difference in satisfaction between a bronze and silver medallist in athletics is significant.

Silver medallists are more likely to think about being one step away from gold. Bronze medallists, on the other hand, are one step away from fourth place, no-medal land, so they're happier than medallist ahead of them. The language of silver medallists focused on losing, i.e. "I almost won" whereas bronze medallists focused on not losing i.e. "At least I did this well". The person worse off (bronze medallist) was consistently happier than the one better off (silver medallist).

Thinking *if only* is what psychologists call *counterfactual thinking*, a mindset in which you think of alternative versions of past events, whether an outcome could have been better or worse. You focus on alternative facts or, more simply put, fiction! Your mind conjures two types of alternative facts, *if only* and *at least*:

*If only I had sent that email when I was supposed to, this wouldn't have happened.*

*If only I'd called the prospect instead of emailing, maybe we wouldn't be in this mess.*

*If only I hadn't said that.*

Thinking thoughts of a better outcome contingent upon a different action taken in the past makes you feel terrible. However, they can also motivate you to improve future performance e.g. "If only I'd asked. Next time I'll ask."

Examples of the second type of alternative facts include:

*At least I didn't run out of petrol on the motorway.*

*At least I made the follow-up call. If I hadn't, the issue would have escalated.*

*At least we met, I can mention it when I email her.*

The *at least* way of thinking gets you to look at how things could have been worse and how, because of your actions, you're better off. *At least* thinking is more comforting and less disheartening than *if only* thinking. Instead of wasting your day ruminating how things could have been better, you can surmount or even circumvent the productivity speedbump through *at least* thinking. What follows is a tool to help you erode your mind's tendency to *if only* thinking.

## The "At Least" Technique

Consider a scenario that is bothering you, a scenario in which you feel the outcome could have been better.

What "bad" thing *might* have prevented you from achieving the outcome you actually got?

What action did you take that prevented that bad thing from happening/enabled you to achieve you actual outcome?

Fill in the gap in this sentence: *At least* [insert what bad thing might have happened that didn't] *which would have been the case if I hadn't* [insert action you took].

Example:

In Rubina's case, she could have charged more from the client she landed but didn't.

*What might have prevented her from winning that client?*
There were extreme train delays, that day. She could have been quite late, which would have flustered her, or worse, she could have completely missed the meeting.

*Action she took to prevent bad thing?*
She took the bus instead of waiting for a train, allowing her to arrive on time for the meeting instead of late or not at all.

*Fill in the gap sentence:*
**At least** she didn't miss the meeting or wasn't late, **which would have been the case if** she hadn't taken the bus.

You should also take the opportunity to use what you've learned to improve future outcomes:

*Three things I can do next time to avoid making the same mistake are...*

Changing your thinking around past events doesn't change the

93

fact that Rubina secured £3000 instead of £3800. But instead of trashing your day with regret, which doesn't solve anything or move you forward in any way, you can declutter your mind. Leave space to be more constructive and creative in the next moment. Stop wasting your time and energy on what might have been and start creating what could be.

When you continually replay the past in the present moment, you relive the anxiety of it. One time while exchanging emails with a client, his response to "How was your day?" was "Trying to enjoy the summer in between these periods of bad weather! Got soaked on Wednesday, can't believe it's August!" At the time of sending this email, the sky was blue and mostly clear. It was t-shirt weather. Yet on a glorious summer day, with his riverfront office, all he could think about was when it rained in the past, making him miserable in the present.

Where do alternative facts show up in your life? How are you labelling yourself or past events in a way that ruins your present?

Now that you're aware of the harmful consequences of alternative facts on your ability and wellbeing, it is a good time to meet a close relative of the self-judgement poisoning your potential.

## That One Annoying Cousin

Self-judgement has a close relative, the annoying Cousin Comparison, who turns up to take things from you. Have you ever thumbed through social feeds when news of a competitor arrested your attention and put you in a foul mood for the rest of the day? Like an annoying cousin who makes you feel terrible, turning up solely because they want something from you, ruminating about competitors steals your concentration, creativity and confidence. You start attacking yourself, thinking about how rubbish you are and how you'll never be able to do

XYZ. Your confidence nosedives and then you wonder if there's any point to doing anything. Sound familiar? This feeling can carry on for days. How can you get anything useful done with Cousin Comparison raiding your house?

## Rear-view Mirror Technique

When you berate yourself for not achieving more, use the Rear-view Mirror Technique to help reconstruct your confidence.

Be aware of how you're feeling. This is a good indicator of whether you're thinking useful thoughts or not.

Next, look back to where you were three, then two and then one year ago and count your accomplishments along the way, no matter how big or small. What hurdles did you jump to get to where you are now? What did you learn? How have you grown?

Make a list of 10 small wins you have achieved in your past year. It all counts in your life's journey.

We're all running our own race. When you breathe your last breath, winning won't matter; it's whether deep down you knew you did the best you could and lived up to your potential. The only person you're competing against is the person looking back at you in the mirror. Let everyone else elbow for second place

## Be your best friend

Keenly aware of how she was limiting her business' growth by depending solely on referrals for the past two years, Evgenia started doing outbound sales activity. After getting zero response from people, she retreated to working on easier tasks, like tweeting quote cards and tweaking her website. But she knew deep down busyness would not grow her business.

Her internal conversation was:

*I'm useless at this.*

*My business will never take off.*

*No one likes my product.*

*They'll say no.*

*I can't make it in business.*

*I should find a proper job.*

Her conversation with a friend went like this:

**Friend:** How many clients have you got?
**Evgenia:** Eleven
**Friend:** How do they feel about your work?
**Evgenia:** They love it, they're very happy.
**Friend:** Would they just say that to you?
**Evgenia:** No.
**Friend:** Just because a few haven't responded doesn't mean no one wants to work with you. This is a little setback. Everyone starts somewhere. Plenty of successful people face rejection, it's normal. Well done for trying and getting out of your comfort zone.

Notice the difference in Evgenia's response versus her friend's response to her suffering? Professor Emeritus of Social Science and Psychology at Stanford University, Albert Bandura[15], says one way of modifying your beliefs in your ability is to simply reduce your stress reaction, in other words, your tendency towards negative chatter and misinterpreting the situation. In other words, keep the Hammer in check.

One way of doing this is be more compassionate towards yourself. There are three steps to cultivating self-compassion according Kristen Neff[16], author of *Self-Compassion: Stop Beating Yourself Up and Leave Insecurity Behind*. Similar to Evghenia's conversation with her best friend, the BEST technique below can help to cultivate more kindness towards yourself.

## The BEST Technique

### *Be your best friend*

Step one is to comfort yourself when you're suffering, as you would with your best friend. Say things like, "You need a good glass of wine after that, well done for trying," or "They would be lucky to have you. This is a minor setback in the grand scheme of things." Focusing on thoughts of compassion silences the Hammer, stopping the steady flow of stress chemicals into your bloodstream.

### *Everyone screws up*

Step two, remind yourself that everyone messes up. You're not the only one who's going through this or who has ever experienced this. Knowing you're not alone comforts you by removing the sting from your particular situation.

### *Silence*

Silence your mind's chatter by getting present so you can objectively observe your experiences, rather than getting caught up in the drumbeat of the Hammer.

### *Thanks*

Move your energy forward by giving thanks for where you are and the opportunities ahead of you.

Instead of kicking yourself when you're down with self-judgement, give yourself a helping hand by using the BEST technique. Instead of drowning in self-doubt, you can move forward with courage.

## Direct your thinking to direct your experience

The more you judge others, the more you judge yourself; the more you judge yourself, the more you judge others. When you rip up the labels you stick onto others, you're also ripping up the labels you stick onto yourself.

To save yourself from your mind's tendency to feast on alternative facts or Cousin Comparison leaching away your wellbeing, make it a daily practice to do your best work, your most important creative work, before consuming (social) media or mail. I know you think you are in control (that's the old confirmation bias talking), but media outlets make money on gaining and keeping your attention. Anything you read is engineered to trigger your commentator, which stifles your creativity.

If you detect a feeling of superiority or inferiority while interacting with others, you are looking through the lens of judgement, which activates the Hammer. When you're aware of your judgement, you can choose to take a breath, activate the Coach, and see the divine in them, which is also in you.

# PRINCIPLE VI

# Unconditionally Accept

*If you surrendered to the air, you could ride it.*
- Toni Morrison, author

*When you learn to accept instead of expect, you'll have fewer disappointments.*
- Robert Fisher, author

*The heart surrenders everything to the moment. The mind judges and holds back.*
- Ram Dass, author, spiritual teacher, clinical psychologist

When I started a new job in Dubai to launch a super-secret product, I foolishly assumed we'd have a nice stretch of time to make a big and special splash.

Three days into the new job and less than four weeks away from launch, the finance director decided the launch target for the new product would be $85,000. No one knew anything about this product. Zero marketing activity had been executed and the market average value for our sort of product was $1500, which meant we had to secure roughly 50 new customers in less than four weeks. The marketing department consisted of me and a colleague picking up the phone and meeting prospects face-to-face. And not everyone you talk to buys immediately. How often do people buy on your timescale? So to secure 50 customers, we would have to develop the interest of at least five times as many prospects. Again, that's 250 prospects within 3.5 weeks for a major product with zero market presence.

After hearing this news, I returned to my desk, mouth agape and short of breath. *This timescale is insanely unreasonable, ridiculously stupid, plucking numbers out of their backside. I should have asked about this company before accepting this job. How could I be so stupid! They're so unprofessional!* For the rest of the day I raged silently in the fumes of fury and frustration. Paralysed by poisonous thoughts, I couldn't do anything productive.

*Why didn't I check the deadline before accepting the job?* Before accepting the job, I had mistakenly assumed the launch was months away. Too enamoured by the opportunity, I didn't ask this crucial question during the interview stage. For the rest of the day, my mind pounded away on a treadmill of dread, fear and injustice.

I went home at 5 pm knowing I couldn't do anything useful or constructive in such a desperate state. I resolved to stop fixating on how things should be and instead concentrate on where I was and what could be.

The next day, after my 6 am swim, I got ready for work in a determined mood. The office was empty when I reached my desk at 8 am. I told myself it didn't matter what would happen in 3.5 weeks. If I lost my job, I knew I could deal with it. *For now, here I am, this is what is.*

## Lifting the Fog

Sitting in the silence, I let out a deep breath and accepted where I was. The fog of anxiety lifted, leaving my mind clear. I asked myself, "What's the best way to approach this? What's the best I can do, right now?" After a few moments of listening to the ether, an idea popped into my head. Something nudged me to make a list of the people I had a warm relationship with, both clients and agencies. Then I listed similar companies, i.e. their competitors. Whilst brainstorming, a broad strategy on how to approach my client segments, followed by tactics, emerged. This idea might seem obvious now, but when the fog of anxiety shrouds your mind, it crowds out any new ideas. When the Hammer is overactive, your brain resorts to habit-loops of ego-fuelled thinking, like blaming and shaming others, instead of taking responsibility.

Unconditionally accepting the situation freed my mind to get on and do the best I possibly could with the given resources. When your mind fights what is, you're blind to all potential solutions.

Accepting what is drops the blinkers blocking your flow. Accepting we were where we were – and that it was okay – gave me the strength to turn it around. Soldiering on, I made upwards of 60 calls a day to set up meetings. For three days of the week I was in back-to-back meetings, returning to my desk after 7 pm.

I was always at my desk on the phone when colleagues straggled in at 9 am. My desk was next to the revenue board and the first thing everyone did when they entered was look up at the numbers. Two weeks passed and the white revenue board still had a big fat zero under "Revenue" next to "$85,000 to go". It was embarrassing. Whenever I looked at the board, a sinking feeling pulled me down, blocking my flow. Sales organisations commonly display revenue boards with either team or individual's numbers as a shame stick to motivate salespeople, but it only discouraged me. Plenty of studies have shown that external incentives are far less effective than internal drivers of performance. I decided to stop looking at that board and instead focus on how many people I could help. I decided to accept this opportunity as a challenge to raise my game and develop strength.

Two weeks into the job, I started enjoying the challenge. I didn't think about the numbers. But there was a moment, at 6 pm on a Tuesday with 1.5 weeks to go, when I looked at the board. We still had $0 in revenue. Fear engulfed me again. *If we didn't hit that target, I'd be out of a job for sure, which meant no visa, which meant deportation.* Across the open plan office I could hear the hum of the marketing team chatting and working away; they were organising a launch party for the product at the Burj Al Arab, that glitzy hotel in Dubai that looks like a sail.

*What if there's no revenue!?!?* My throat felt like a boa constrictor had wrapped its slimy body around it. I was frozen with worry, physically shaking – that only happens when I'm really scared. After pacing and breathing, I returned to a state that allowed me to drive home safely. That evening I reminded myself to accept the situation. I had done my best. *Come what may.*

At the end of week three, at 5 pm on Friday afternoon, my first inbound call came in:

> **Prospect:** Hello Anis, Sandra here from Shore Capital.
> **Anis:** Hey Sandra, great to hear from you. How can I help you?
> **Prospect:** Is the sponsorship still available?
> **Anis:** At the moment, yes, but we do have others interested. (Five companies had expressed interest, but Shore were the first to call.)
> **Prospect:** Great, then I'd like to confirm it please. So that's £50,000, right?

Monday morning came around, the phones were ringing like wedding church bells:

> "$15,000 for the gatefold. Booked, thank you."

> "$25,000 for the wrap, confirmed. I'll send you the printing specs."

> "$50,000 confirmed for your sponsorship; how many tickets do you need for the launch?"

> "$10,000 for 2 pages, confirmed."

Halfway through week three, as our non-sales colleagues staggered in, they looked up at board in wide-eyed amazement.

Target: $85,000

Revenue: $194,250

To Go: $0

Between the two of us, we eventually delivered over $250,000, almost three times our target.

Had I continued wallowing in "this is not fair" mode, I highly doubt I would have delivered results. If your ego-mind is occupied trying to prove yourself right, you shirk responsibility when things go wrong.

It was a stressful time and I'm well aware there are people going through far worse. But we are all running our own race, aren't we? Whether you're working for yourself or for an organization, there will be many times you feel the odds are stacked against you. As an entrepreneur, this could emerge as mounting bills or concerns about where your next client will come from. As a stressed salesperson, it could be your employer's unreasonable targets, a lack of resources or a constantly changing incentive structure. Suffering is suffering. It's all relative to a person's life. Times of stress are gifts to help you rise higher and become a better version of you. Challenges are opportunities to flex your mental and spiritual muscles.

As Esther Hicks says, "When you argue for your limitations you get to keep them." Ranting may make you feel better for a moment, but it doesn't change anything. Unless you keep ranting, which will just feed your anger. In non-life-threatening situations, acting from anger leads to regret and outcomes are rarely beneficial. If you always aim to be right, you'll never be happy.

## The Burden of Being Right

In testing circumstances, ruminating about what's bad and fixating on being right can hold you back. It's a terrible burden to bear and won't help you take the necessary action to turn things around. Blaming and shaming others for the situation is like your car being stuck in the mud and stepping on the gas full throttle to escape. Blame only digs a deeper groove into the mud, making it even harder to escape.

The situation might not be great. It might be completely unfair. But if you can't accept where you are, you won't see what could be. You will miss opportunities because you're too busy looking at what's wrong. This psychological lack of attention is called perceptual blindness [17]. There's a famous gorilla experiment where participants were asked to watch a video and count how many times a basketball was passed. After the event, they were asked, "How many of you noticed the gorilla?" Approximately 50% failed to notice the gorilla walk onto the stage, thump its chest and then walk off.

A mind focused on the negative can't achieve a positive outcome. When you resist your current circumstances, you only hurt yourself.

## Release the obstacle

There's a wonderful quote by holocaust survivor Viktor Frankl in his book *Man's Search for Meaning*[18] on acceptance:

> We had to teach the despairing men, that it did not really matter what we expected from life, but rather what life expected from us. We needed to stop asking about the meaning of life, and instead to think of ourselves as those who were being questioned by life – daily and hourly. Our answer must consist, not in talk and meditation but in right action and right conduct.

To be clear, surrender does not mean giving up. Accepting what is does not mean you're endorsing dire conditions or bad behaviours nor does it mean becoming a doormat for other people. It means giving up the resistance blinding you to solutions. It means making space to receive inspiration. And it means you value getting results above your ego's need to be right.

*To the ego mind, surrender is about giving up. To the spiritual mind surrender is about giving in and receiving.*

- Marianne Williamson

Maintaining resistance reinforces the obstacle or opposing force; the more you resist, the stronger the opponent becomes. Remember that law, for every action there is an equal and opposite reaction? In rugby and American football, players crash head and shoulders into each other, then push. And push. And push. The harder they push, the greater the resistance from the opponent. But if one side suddenly stopped pushing and stood aside, their opponent would comically tumble forward.

During one of my *Build Resilience & Restore Balance* workshops, one attendee was stressed out about his boss dumping work on him at the last minute. He felt it was completely unreasonable and unacceptable for the task at hand. His stress hindered his ability to perform to the best of his ability. Preventing last minute work dumps is important to address but let's start with the immediate situation. When I probed, he said:

Anis:  What was going through your head?
Attendee:  That this has been dumped on me last minute and there's not enough time. It made me stressed and I couldn't focus.
Anis:  You wanted the situation to be different?
Attendee:  Yes, I wanted more time.
Anis:  What if you could shift your thinking to, *this is what it is, let me make the best of it?*
Attendee:  Then my boss will think he can keep dumping stuff last minute on me and it's unfair.
Anis:  How is fighting and resisting it helping you?
Attendee:  It's not.
Anis:  If you could accept the situation for a moment, how

could you make the best of it?

Attendee: I could do a good job for the client.

Anis: What else?

Attendee: Negotiate a pay rise with my boss.

When you accept what is, the wall of resistance disappears and the realm of possibility re-emerges.

In the Mindfulness Acceptance Insight Commitment programme for Chinese Athletes [19], a critical step to attaining peak performance is accepting any emotions you are feeling, accepting where you are. *Accept everything is as it is.* By acknowledging the situation as it is, you can see what action or decisions to take from a place of stillness

## Think Inches, Not Miles

To move beyond acceptance and make progress, focus on achieving minor milestones instead of moving mountains. After a perceived failure, nothing motivates you more than small wins. Makena, the sustainable consultant you met in a previous chapter, wasn't doing her regular outbound sales activities. The idea of reaching out to twenty people a month paralysed her. When she realised it was only one-a-day, she laughed. Two weeks later when I checked how she was getting on with her one-a-day target, she was actually reaching out to three or four prospects a day. Achieving daily small wins gives you a hit of dopamine, making you feel great and motivating you to do more

The research [20] of Teresa Amabile, Director of Research at Harvard and author of *The Progress Principle: Using Small Wins to Ignite Joy, Engagement and Creativity at Work,* demonstrates that the most powerful driver of motivation is making meaningful progress. After examining the events and diary entries of thousands of workdays in real-time, she found the single greatest mechanism driving a sense of achievement was making consistent and meaningful progress.

When deciding on next steps, people mistakenly focus on the result or outcome they want, which makes it daunting to start at all. Instead, slice the desired outcome into minute activities you need to complete to get there. For example, one client wasted hours a day following up with clients. He wanted to find a better way to systematise his admin work, but the thought of it was overwhelming so he kept suffering. After we worked together to chop up his activities into tiny steps, he mapped out a process, most of which he outsourced, saving him several hours a day.

Focus on achieving those tiny wins so you make steady progress. As you achieve each miniature milestone, you start feeling successful. Mastery experiences, moments where you experience wins, is one of the most powerful ways of increasing your belief and confidence.

## Who should you become?

Being successful is not about creating the perfect path or pursuing perfection but learning to accept adversity and dance with difficulty. Accepting what is, as it comes, liberates you. Instead of being a victim, you rise and become the victor. When you meet adversity, ask yourself, "Who is this situation asking me to become?" Be silent, listen to the whispers, then act.

# PRINCIPLE VII

# Let Go

*Grasping at things can only yield one of two results:*
*either the thing you are grasping at disappears, or you yourself*
*disappear. It is only a matter of which occurs first.*
- Goenka, meditation teacher

*Develop the witness attitude and you will find your own experience that*
*detachment brings control.*
- Nisargadatta Maharaj, spiritual teacher

*Having rests on giving and not getting.*
- Helen Schucman, author of A Course In Miracles

Sipping mulled wine on a frosty winter evening, I navigated the crowd of a networking event to join a huddle. The host introduced me to the people in the group which comprised an accountant, an estate agent, a locksmith and a network marketer.

After ten minutes of polite chatter passed, Surreya from Freedom Living approached me.

**Surreya:** So, you're a salesperson?

**Anis:** In my former life, in my corporate career, yes.

**Surreya:** You should come join me as a wellness entrepreneur. I represent Lovely Wellness, a network marketing company. You can earn lots of money on the side. I got a check in the post last month from a meeting I had with someone last year. It was amazing! I forgot all about it and it just arrived out of the blue. You get to work from home, work your own hours. You get to grow a team – I already have one person working for me. When you build your team and get to another level, they give you a car. You can earn money on the side to build your dream.

**Anis:** That sounds lovely. Thank you for the offer, but I'm quite happy with what I'm doing.

**Surreya:** But this is a side business. You can keep doing your job and run this and earn extra money. It's easy to set up…

Her pitch went on for a good ten minutes. I squirmed and tried changing the subject to wellness practices and then to food, but every time she sharply u-turned to the earning potential gained from joining her team. Other than my job title, she knew nothing about me and showed zero interest in finding out.

Surreya was maniacally focused on one thing: making money. Successfully recruiting me would bring her a share of my potential sales of Lovely Wellness products, which is why she didn't want me to get away. In her mind, me walking away was equivalent to a loss for her. Stressed states bias us towards selfish behaviour [21], especially in personal and emotionally intense situations. The more cortisol circulating in your body, the more selfish and egoistic your behaviour, because you're operating in survival mode.

## Splintered Attention

Setting achievable goals is important for motivating and inspiring you, but fastening yourself to a specific outcome while engaging with others splinters your attention and activates the Hammer. For Surreya to achieve a favourable outcome, she didn't have to change the environment or me. The only change she had to make was in her mind. When you change your mind's projection, you change the direction of the conversation. Change begins with you. By freeing yourself of fear-based thoughts, which result in selfish motives, you leave space to allow connection, trust and sales.

*You cannot give when you're trying to take.*

When my wife and I visited Vancouver, we went on the Capilano Suspension Bridge. It measures 140 metres and hovers 70 metres above a river, a height equivalent to the top of London's Westminster Abbey (that place where royal weddings happen). Standing before the bridge, a hand on each side rail, I was petrified. But with each tiny step across the wooden planks, my fear abated. This is a good metaphor for a sales scenario; without building a bridge of trust, plank by plank, your client will not cross the valley of fear to risk working with you or purchasing your product.

Ayesha, another network marketer, faced Surreya's dilemma of selling her products and recruiting others to sell for her. We worked on helping her cultivate *letting go* during conversations with people. Instead of selling or recruiting, she shifted to being her friendly, curious self, with no hidden agenda. She got to know more people, exploring how to add value to their lives. Instead of people disappearing after initial conversations, she achieved greater engagement and eventually grew her team and her sales.

When you engage from a detached place, others intuitively know you don't have a hidden agenda, that you have their best interests at heart. You know why? Because you do. When you let go of the outcome, your attention is no longer splintered. It's focused. On them. When prospective clients feel you have their best interests at heart, you will build trust and grow your business and referrals.

*When you're attached, you're repelling; when you're detached you're compelling.*

## Does This Mean I Don't Care?

Letting go of the need to achieve a goal doesn't mean you don't care. It means you're open to giving your best in the current moment. Excellence happens now, not in the future. You have a target to hit, goals to achieve and results to deliver, but you can't give your best now when your mind is focused on the pressure of achieving a future outcome.

You don't do your best work when you're stressed; stress

depletes your working memory, which is why you suddenly forget critical bits of information during conversations, like market research or happy clients. Don't be owned by the outcome. It doesn't mean avoiding things, it means being where you are rather than distracted by where you wish you were.

*Sometimes letting things go is an act of far greater power than defending or hanging on.*

– Eckhart Tolle

You might be wondering, doesn't detachment remove the emotional urgency, love, passion and drive of working on a mission? Quite the opposite! Releasing yourself from the burden of competition allows you to dwell in the space where you have the most power, where you do your best work, where you can be of the greatest service, which is now. Remember, you are where your attention is. When you're no longer concerned about an outcome, all your attention can be directed to being of service right now.

Imagine you're a Bentley salesperson and the Queen of England walks into your dealership. Are you going to launch into your sales pitch so you can ultimately hit your targets? No, you'd want to give her the best experience ever! It's about thinking, *wow, this person has walked into my showroom, how can I give them the best experience?* Treat every encounter, every conversation, with that thought in mind. Doing so makes you focus on the present moment instead of fixating on hitting a target or making money.

## What Where Why technique

*What's on my mind right now? Am I focused on providing a great experience or am I distracted by my own thoughts or getting a specific result?*

113

Be honest with yourself.

*Where will I direct my mind right now in this encounter? How can I keep my mind focused on providing the best experience?*

*Why do I do what I do? What's my bigger why?*
This helps you address your values and purpose and steer your intention in the right direction, no matter what the outcome.

## Tombstone technique

This might sound morbid but reflecting on death brings to the forefront what really matters when you're alive. Pondering your last days on earth can help you realise that closing a sale doesn't matter, nor does making more money. What matters is the impact you create, the lives you touch and the people you transform through your actions, right now.

*Once you learn how to die, you learn how to live.*

– Mitch Albom

Consumer culture thrives on your fear of missing out and dependency on social validation. When you're constantly concerned with external validation, you rarely cultivate inner strength. When you reflect on the bigger concerns like meaning, purpose and values, instead of getting sucked into junk values of greed, convenience and consumption, fears fall away. When you free yourself of the ego's chatter that keeps you small and listen to the whispers that come from within, you can start growing your impact.

*Remembering that I'll be dead soon is the most important tool I've ever encountered to help me make the big choices in life. Because almost everything — all external expectations, all pride, all fear of embarrassment or failure – these things just fall away in the face of death, leaving only what is truly important. Remembering that you are going to die is the best way I know to avoid the trap of thinking you have something to lose.*

- Steve Jobs

# Your Guilted Armor

I recently received an email from an entrepreneur that said the following:

*Anis, I bought a ticket to attend your session this afternoon, but I arrived at 4 pm instead of 2 pm. I'm so frustrated with myself. When are you running another one?*

In his follow-up email he repeated how frustrated he was with himself. His constant commentator was still replaying that mistake in his head, ceaselessly nipping at his conscience. Guilt is not only a popular weapon of the commentator, but also a common cultural weapon of control. Your commentator uses guilt to beat us down.

How many times have you started your day with a brilliant plan for sales activities only to have it crumble away before your eyes? You allocated hours, itemised follow-ups and detailed customer concerns to action before they explode into big problems. You start by turning on your laptop and replying to email. Maybe you make a quick call and check something online. Then it's time for a cup of tea after which you very quickly tweak your website. Might as well, right? You're online anyway. You make a quick call to a colleague you've been meaning to catch up with and remember you have to check that Facebook group to see if anything interesting popped up. Suddenly it's 3:45 pm. How is it that time already? You haven't even started on your core tasks you set out in the morning!

Now you're wearing guilt like a rusty suit of armour. *How could I be so stupid. Why do I always do this? Why can't I do anything right?* Off your mind goes, like greyhounds at the racetrack. It's impossible to perform at your best when you're weighed down with a suit of guilt armor.

As someone who used to sport a wardrobe of guilted armor for all seasons, I can share a way to free you of the burden. You could call it a way of Marie Kondo'ing your wardrobe of guilt armor, and there's science to prove its effectiveness.

## Self-Inflicted Wounds

What is procrastination? The common perception is procrastinators are lazy, but is that true? How productive are you when you procrastinate? Personally, I've alphabetised books, vacuumed the flat and cleaned the cat's drinking fountain when I was supposed to be writing this book. Procrastination is not laziness; it's a stress response and a breakdown in your self-regulatory behaviour, the domain of your Coach.

How do you feel after procrastinating? Awful? Filled with guilt and self-loathing? These harmful negative emotions weigh you down, sucking away your confidence and stopping you from doing the things you should be doing. Next time you find yourself procrastinating, the most powerful thing you can do is eliminate the toxic feelings associated with it. Shedding your guilted armour mentally frees you up to do the hard things that need to be done.

So, how do you remove your guilted armour? The key is self-forgiveness. Here's how Professor Robert D. Enright, a prominent researcher on forgiveness, defines self-forgiveness:

> Self-forgiveness is a willingness to abandon self-resentment in the face of one's own acknowledged objective wrong, while fostering compassion, generosity, and love toward oneself.

You have to let go of the hate you bear for that thing you did wrong or that thing you haven't done at all. Hating yourself for not following-up or for the mistake you made won't change anything. People make mistakes all the time. You did the best you could, so be kind and loving to yourself.

You can change how you do things in the future. Ask yourself, "What can I do right now to make up for this mistake?" And instead of isolating yourself as a terrible screw-up, change your perspective by taking a helicopter view and see and know that you are human, that we all make mistakes. Self-forgiveness is about shifting from destructive to constructive thought patterns.

A study from Carleton University's psychology department [22] examined the association between self-forgiveness and procrastination and arrived at some interesting findings that could set you free. First you need to acknowledge that procrastination is a transgression against yourself. It's a form of self-harm or self-sabotage because not doing what needs to be done affects your well-being.

Here are three instances where self-forgiveness can help shed your guilted armour:

1. Mistakes: You turn up for an appointment at 4 pm when it actually started at 2 pm.

2. Unconscious action: You snap at a loved one, a colleague or a random person because you were in your ego.

3. Procrastination: You faff on social media instead of working out or doing other mission critical activities.

There are many more areas where guilt weighs you down, especially if you were raised in an environment where guilt was used as a behaviour moderation tool, so it becomes part of your constant commentator's habitual dialogue.

*To overcome your mind's tendency to make you feel bad, download your*

*Constant Commentator Coping Strategies worksheet here http://anisqizilbash.com/book-resources/)*

## Am I letting myself off the hook?

You might be thinking, *won't I just keep procrastinating if I let myself off the hook by forgiving myself?* Such thinking implies that you have to be hard on yourself, think awful thoughts about yourself, to keep yourself from messing up again. How's that working out for you? And what's a better use of your time – spending all afternoon berating yourself for past errors so you feel awful and demotivated, or doing something useful in the present moment, like making that call or starting your creative project?

When you finally do the thing you've been procrastinating, how do you think you will feel? Science shows you'll feel pretty good because you ticked something off your list, giving you hit of dopamine. That's the motivational drug. You activate a virtuous cycle in which you want to go on and do the next task.

Holding on to the past by replaying what you should have done and how useless you were renders you powerless and hopeless in the present. Freeing yourself from the past by letting go dodges hours of despair, while giving you the space to do the important stuff and boldly step towards achieving your goals and growing your impact.

### Drop the Weight Technique

Did you mess up recently, or is procrastination giving you guilt indigestion? Let's work with that. Using a pen and paper, walk through the following four steps to course correct and do that thing you should have done.

> *I made a mistake and I acknowledge feeling guilt is mostly harming myself.*

*I forgive myself for _____, we all make mistakes.*

*I'm doing the best I can. I will do better next time.*
*The action I can take now to improve the situation*
*is_____?*
List 3 options, then pick one and give yourself five
minutes to get started immediately.

*From my top priority today, the tiny step I will do now to*
*move forward is_____?*
The tiny step must only take 10 minutes to do. Your
objective is purely getting started. List 3 options, then
pick one and get started immediately.

This Drop the Weight technique helps you let go of the guilt
you're holding on to, and then do something constructive about
it. Building on that momentum, you guide yourself to move onto
other priorities.

## Direct your outcomes

Wearing your guilted armour after you've messed up doesn't
make you a brave warrior. Guilt punishes you and doesn't make
anything better. Quite the opposite, it's a destructive thought
pattern which fuels more destructive behaviour. To switch from
destructive to constructive behaviour so you can be your brilliant
self all day, walk through the Drop the Weight technique to guide
your thinking. When you let go of the weight pulling you down,
you can take action to lift yourself up.

# Rise

*Yesterday I was clever, so I wanted to change the world. Today I am wise,*
*so I am changing myself.*
- Rumi, Sufi mystic

*Your legacy is not what you leave behind, it's the lives you touch going*
*forward.*
- Maya Angelou, author and activist

*Be bold and mighty forces will come to your aid.*
- Basil King, author

After three years of intense study, a novice monk arrived at his teacher's residence, excitedly tossing ideas around the latest ideas in metaphysics, Buddhism and non-duality. He felt well prepared for the extensive questioning in the exam awaiting him. He lightly rapped the door.

"Enter" said his teacher. The novice eagerly scuffled in.
After a pause, his teacher said, "I have one question."
"Yes master, I am ready."
"In the doorway, as you entered, were the flowers to the left or to the right of the umbrella?

The novice racked his brain but could not recall where the flowers were. He left his master's residence with his head hung in shame and the knowledge that many more years of study awaited him.

Like the novice monk, we don't notice the flowers in our life. While technology elevates our ability to trade and connect, our attachment to screens steals the present moment away from us. Our addiction to distraction is a result of a hyperactive Hammer and idle Coach. When thoughts of fear, scarcity and limitation weigh heavier in your mind than thoughts of love, abundance and limitlessness, you'll never do the things that will make the difference in your life and for those you love.

Embodying these seven principles won't change people or

situations. They will, however, help you rise above the swamp of limiting thoughts and destructive distractions. They will help you rise above the dense, dark, fog of fear and scarcity to a place of light, love and abundance, where you act with power instead of weakness, where you're reflective instead of reflexive, where you're bold instead of timid. When you act from a place of power, your actions set a new cause in motion to produce different effects. You change your life not through lofty ideas but humble action.

To change others and your environment, you must start with changing yourself. When you change yourself, you show people how to treat you. After learning to manage her stress and challenging the constant commentator that kept her to silent in meetings and combative with colleagues, one client said, "I have changed their behaviour towards me."

It doesn't matter what mistake you made, what you should or should not have done; no matter how much you're tested and how long and dark your days feel, there is always power is inside you. Every moment you have access to infinite power, you just have to decide to access it and rise. A lotus flower is born in darkness, but it flowers in the light.

As darkness is the absence of light, fear is the absence of love. When you recognise fear in others, be it through their hostility or obstinate behaviour, recognise it as the absence of love instead of taking offense. When you meet fear with fear it results in conflict and gives fear more power, causing more suffering. When you extinguish the darkness of fear in others with the light of love, you demonstrate to yourself that your own fear can also be extinguished with light.

*Your playing small does not serve the world. There's nothing enlightened about shrinking so that other people won't feel insecure around you.*

- Marianne Williamson

Being bold doesn't mean being arrogant, superior or obnoxious. Boldness is making phone calls even though you're afraid; knocking on another door after failing spectacularly on the previous one; doing something you've never done; calling that dream client even though your knees are shaking; raising your fees and charging what you're worth; putting yourself forward for a contest or speaking gig; mastering a new skill; breaking a bad habit. Boldness is a quiet inner strength, not noisy external bluster.

Using the seven principles, you rise above the limiting beliefs and illusory ideas pulling you down. You embody your authentic self. It's being unapologetically you. There's a natural steadiness in your speech, strength in your actions, certainty in your energy. To others, these traits may appear bold, but this is the real you, no longer in the shadow of past conditioning. Boldness isn't something you're born with, either. It's something you cultivate through consistent courageous action.

*Courage is the most important of all the virtues because without courage, you can't practice any other virtue consistently.*

– Maya Angelou

By giving your full attention to each moment, you bring your fully engaged self to the doing, you work in concert with an intelligent force far greater than the ego mind. By practicing the principles in this book, you will peel off the layers of conditioning weighing you down and rise through the murky waters of fear and stress. You can flower into your brilliant bold self.

Anger, anxiety, and fear fall away when you allow each person and moment you meet to lift you to become more of who you are. When you refuse to lie hidden in the dark depths of fear, you rise. I challenge you, from this day on, with everyone you meet and each challenge you greet, to replace all the darkness of fear with light. Use it to help you rise.

# THE SEVEN PRINCIPLES OF MINDFUL SELLING

### MAKE SPACE TO WATCH
Stop getting caught up *in* your thoughts by making space to *watch* your thoughts.

### IMPOSE YOUR INTENTION
A fearful mind alienates others. Shift your intention from selling to serving.

### NOTICE THE GOOD
In the absence of all that is bad, the presence of all that is good appears.

### DON'T ASSUME
Assumptions close doors. Questions open doors.

### FREE YOURSELF
The more you judge others, the more you judge yourself. Be kinder to yourself.

### UNCONDITIONALLY ACCEPT
When you accept what is, resistance disappears and opportunity reappears.

### LET GO
When you're attached, you're repelling. When you're detached, you're compelling.

# ABOUT THE AUTHOR

For the past 20 years, Anis has been in the business of changing hearts and minds, getting people to take action to achieve the success they desire. At first this took the form of a corporate sales career, which gave her the opportunity to help all sorts of people around the world take action to move towards their goals. She developed an approach to fit her socially awkward, quiet persona; because she hated selling so much, the only way she could thrive was to be of service.

Against the backdrop of this career, she dealt with truckloads of emotional baggage – decades of depression, despair and disorder. Learning to surmount personal struggles and assembling a suite of tools and systems in the process fuelled a desire to help alleviate the suffering of others.

After leaving the corporate world, she went on to teach her system to people who fear and hate selling with Mindful Sales Training. By applying the same skills used to change hearts and minds in corporate sales and tapping into her own experiences, she's helped individuals let go of their limiting beliefs and behaviours to access reserves of untapped potential.

**If you found this book useful, please leave a review to help others find it.**

To book Anis to speak at your next conference or bulk purchase copies of this book contact her at:

Email: a@anisqizilbash.com ~ Website: anisqizilbash.com

# Bibliography

[11] Momentary Interruptions Can Derail the Train of Thought, *Journal of Experimental Psychology,* Erik Altman et al.

[2] Bandura, A. (1994). Self-efficacy. In V. S. Ramachaudran (Ed.), *Encyclopedia of Human Behavior* (Vol. 4, pp. 71-81). New York: Academic Press. (Reprinted in H. Friedman [Ed.], *Encyclopedia of Mental Health.* San Diego: Academic Press, 1998).

[3] B. Keith Payne, et al, (2016), Replicable Effects of Primes on Human Behavior, *Journal of Experimental Psychology: General*, Vol. 145, No. 10, 1269–127

[4] Marcus E. Raichlea, et al. (2007) A default mode of brain function: A brief history of an evolving idea, *NeuroImage*, 37, 1083 – 1090

[5] Siegel, Daniel J. *Mindsight: the New Science of Personal Transformation.* Bantam Books, 2011 (Kindle location 522 of 6984)

[6] Sapolsky, Robert M. *Behave: the Biology of Humans at Our Best and Worst.* Vintage, 2018 Pp. 35

[7] Taylor, Jill Bolte Ph. D. *My Stroke of Insight A Brain Scientist's Personal Journey.* Hodder & Stoughton General Division, 2011 Pp 147.

[8] Emmons, RA, (2003), *Counting Blessings Versus Burdens: An Experimental Investigation of Gratitude and Subjective Well-Being in Daily Life*, Journal of Personality and Social Psychology, Vol.84, No.2, 377–389

[9] https://selfdeterminationtheory.org/SDT/documents/2000_R yanDeci_SDT.pdf

[10] Deci, Koestner, and Ryan, Meta-Analytic Review of Experiments Examining the Effects of Extrinsic Rewards on Intrinsic Motivation, *Psychological Bulletin* 1999, Vol. 125, No. 6, 627-668

[11] Covington, M, The Self-Worth Theory of Achievement Motivation: Findings and Implications, *The Elementary School Journal* 1984, Vol. 85, No. 1

[13] Dweck, Carol S. *Mindset: How You Can Fulfil Your Potential.* Robinson, 2012. Kindle, Chapter 2  location 156 of 6677

[14] Medvec, Victoria Husted, Madey, Scott, Gilovich, Thomas, (1995) When Less Is More: Counterfactual Thinking and Satisfaction Among Olympic Medalists, Journal *of Personality and Social Psychology*, 69, pp 603 – 610

[15] Bandura, A. (1994).  Self-efficacy.  In V. S. Ramachaudran (Ed.), *Encyclopedia of Human Behavior* (Vol. 4, pp. 71-81).  New York: Academic Press.

[16] Neff, Kristin. *Self Compassion: Stop Beating Yourself up and Leave Insecurity Behind* Yellow Kite, 2015 Kindle location 575 4335

[17] Simons, Daniel, (2012, September), But Did You See the Gorilla?  The  Problem  With  Inattentional  Blindness, https://www.smithsonianmag.com/

[18] Frankl, Viktor E. *Man's Search for Meaning: the Classic Tribute to*

*Hope from the Holocaust.* Rider, 2008.Pp 85

[19] Gang-yan Si, et al, (2016) Mindfulness Training Programme for Chinese Athletes and Its Effectiveness. Baltzell, Amy. *Mindfulness and Performance.* Cambridge University Press, 2017. Pp. 248

[20] Amabile, Teresa, (2011, May) The Power of Small Wins, https://hbr.org

[21] Sapolsky, Robert M. *Behave: the Biology of Humans at Our Best and Worst.* Vintage, 2018 pp 132

[22] Michael J.A. Wohl, et al., (2010) I forgive myself, now I can study: How self-forgiveness for procrastinating can reduce future procrastination. *Personality and Individual Differences* 48, 803–808

Printed in Great Britain
by Amazon